D1319666

AMERICAN EDUCATION

Its Men

Ideas

and

Institutions

Apprenticeship
&
Apprenticeship Education
in
Colonial
New England & New York

Robert Francis Seybolt

ARNO PRESS & THE NEW YORK TIMES
New York * 1969

Reprint edition 1969 by Arno Press, Inc.

*

Library of Congress Catalog Card No. 70-89230

*

Reprinted from a copy in Teachers College Library

*

Manufactured in the United States of America

Editorial Note

AMERICAN EDUCATION: *Its Men, Institutions and Ideas* presents selected works of thought and scholarship that have long been out of print or otherwise unavailable. Inevitably, such works will include particular ideas and doctrines that have been outmoded or superseded by more recent research. Nevertheless, all retain their place in the literature, having influenced educational thought and practice in their own time and having provided the basis for subsequent scholarship.

Lawrence A. Cremin
Teachers College

Apprenticeship

&

Apprenticeship Education

in

Colonial

New England & New York

Apprenticeship & Apprenticeship Education in Colonial New England & New York

ROBERT FRANCIS SEYBOLT

ASSISTANT PROFESSOR OF EDUCATION, UNIVERSITY OF WISCONSIN;
SOMETIME RESEARCH SCHOLAR IN EDUCATION, TEACHERS COLLLEGE
COLUMBIA UNIVERSITY

SUBMITTED IN PARTIAL FULFILLMENT OF THE
REQUIREMENTS FOR THE DEGREE OF DOCTOR OF PHILOSOPHY
IN THE FACULTY OF PHILOSOPHY
COLUMBIA UNIVERSITY

PUBLISHED BY
Teachers College, Columbia University
NEW YORK CITY
1917

CONTENTS

Apprenticeship and Apprenticeship Education in Colonial New England and New York

CHAPTER I

THE APPRENTICESHIP SYSTEM IN ENGLAND

THE essential characteristics of the practice of apprenticeship in the American colonies were determined by English gild and municipal legislation of the thirteenth and fourteenth centuries. To understand the colonial practice it is necessary, therefore, to know its historical antecedents, and for this purpose a somewhat detailed account of English apprenticeship will be given. Later chapters will show its reproduction and continuation in colonial New England and New York.

It is from gild ordinances, statutes, and indentures that we get our knowledge of apprenticeship. Available records reveal the fact that apprenticeship was practiced in England in the thirteenth century; one of the earliest references appears in the ordinance of the Lorimers of London in 1261, forbidding one master to entice away another's apprentice, and fixing the term of service at ten years: "Item ce nul fortreie autre emprentiz, ne autri sergeaunt, dedenz son term, ne sul emprentiz receyve a mendre terme ce a X aunz, et ove XXX soulz au meyns; et jurge ydonqe lemprentiz de tenir les purveaunces en cest escrit conteniz."[1] From an early statute, dated 1275, we learn that the names of apprentices were kept on a paper in the Chamber of the

[1] Liber Custumarum, I, 78.

Guildhall.[2] The enrollment of an apprentice within the first year of his term was strongly insisted on by the municipal authorities, every freeman on admission binding himself by oath to see that any apprentice of his was so enrolled.[3] It was also required that the Guildhall preserve copies of the indenture, or articles of agreement between master and apprentice. The records refer frequently to the "paper of apprentices"[4] upon which "ingresses" and "egresses" were recorded, and to "a certain writing indented made between them (master and apprentice), which he (the apprentice) brought before the chamberlain."[5] One of the earliest references to apprentices in the city records occurs in the year 1279 or 1280, when the ordinances for regulating the trade of fishmongers were amended. Among these ordinances we find some relating to apprentices to the following effect: that henceforth no one shall take more than two or three apprentices at most, according to his ability to support them; that no one shall take an apprentice for a less term than seven years; that the master and the apprentice come to the Guildhall and cause the agreement and the term to

[2] Cal. Letter-Book D, n. 37. "Eodem anno quaedam libertas in Londoniis fuit provisa, ut apprenticiorum nomina abbreviaretur in papirio camerae Gildaulae et eorum nomina qui libertatem dictae civitatis amere voluerent, in eodem papirio insererentur; et cujus nomen non fuit in dicto papirio libertate civitatis privaretur."

We find the "old paper of apprentices of 4 Ed. I" mentioned several times in the 14th century (Cal. Let. Bk. D, 65, 151).

[3] Cal. Let. Bk. D, 195–96. "Oath of Freemen (1275): Ye shall swear that ye shall be faithful and loyal unto our lord the King, King of England . . . and the franchises and customs of the City ye shall maintain according to your power. . . . Ye shall take no apprentice for less than seven years, and ye shall cause him to be enrolled as such within the first year of your covenant, and at the end of his term, if he has well and loyally served you, you shall cause his egress to be enrolled. . . . And ye shall take no apprentice unless he be a free man and not a bondsman. All of which points aforesaid ye shall well and truly keep, so God you help and all his saints."

[4] Cal. Let. Bk. D, 96–179. "His ingress appears in the paper of apprenticeships of the aforesaid Ward, anno 28 Edward I." "His ingress appears in the second paper of apprentices in the Ward of Walebrok, anno 28, Edward I."

[5] Cal. Let. Bk. D, 96–179. One of these reads as follows: "the said Hugh (the apprentice) proffered before the Chamberlain a certain writing indented of his apprenticeship, sealed with the seal of the said William (master)."

be enrolled, and also to do the same at the end of the term, unless it is dissolved by the death of one or the other. Further, that if the master die within the term, the apprentice shall come to the Guildhall, and do as he shall be ordered before he do anything of the trade; and lastly, that those who are already apprentices shall do no work after Sunday next, until such time as their masters shall come to the Guildhall and cause their covenant and term to be enrolled.[6] In September, 1300, an Act was passed by the Mayor and the Aldermen to the effect that the names of all apprentices who thenceforth failed to be entered by their masters "on the paper" within their first year should be enrolled on a certain schedule to be produced at the next Husting before the Mayor and Aldermen, with the view to the defaulting apprentices being fined at the discretion of the Chamberlain and two Aldermen specially elected for that purpose.[7] Subsequent records give abundant evidence of the enforcement of this Act.[8]

The rules prescribed for apprenticeship among the fishmongers were afterwards applied to other trades. Thus, among a long series of ordinances (presumably of the year 1312–1313) we find the following: (1) that thenceforth no person shall receive an apprentice unless he himself be free of the city, and cause their covenant to be enrolled, of whatever condition such apprentice may be; (2) that no apprentice after fully serving his term, shall follow his trade in the city before he shall have been sworn of the freemen and thereupon enrolled; (3) that no apprentice shall be received for a less term than seven years, according to the ancient usage.[9] The matter of fact manner in which ap-

[6] Liber Albus, I, 383–84.   [7] Cal. Let. Bk. C, 78. Liber Custumarum, 93.
[8] Cal. Let. Bk. B, 146. A record under the year 1305 reads: "Thomas de Kydeminstre, draper and hosier, came before John le Blound, Mayor, John de Wangrave, and Richard Poterel, Chamberlain, and made fine with the Commonalty for payment of half a mark for a trespass committed touching his apprentice Walter, son of William de Beverlee, taverner, not being enrolled within a year, according to the custom of the City and his oath; to be paid within a fortnight."
[9] Liber Albus, I, 272.

prenticeship is mentioned, and the frequent use of the phrase "according to the ancient usage" presuppose that it was a common practice, and that it must have been in use for some length of time. Further, it shows that apprentices were so frequently employed by Londoners that legislation concerning them was necessary. Most of the London gilds seem to have adopted apprenticeship by 1350, for rules regulating it are common at that date.[10]

The gilds early recognized the custom of taking apprentices. They saw the advantages in compelling all craftsmen to go through a course of training before being admitted to the trade as masters, and as time went on, they sought to effect this by legislation. The content of the records indicates, however, that this prerequisite was probably never completely enforced. Some of the ordinances, drawn up by the various London crafts and confirmed by the Mayor, admitted the attestation of sufficient skill by the craft officials as an alternative to apprenticeship.[11] In many cases they speak of the freedom of the trade as a thing that could be inherited,[12] or bought.[13] But, apprenticeship came gradually to be adopted as the most usual method of entering a craft, and by 1400 was practiced by most gilds, and required by most towns.

[10] An examination of the records for the years 1309–13 shows that 415 apprentices acknowledged themselves bound to at least fifty different crafts or trades (Cal. Let. Bk. D, 96–169).

[11] Memorials, 234. Ordinance of the White Tawyers, 1346: "that no one who has not been an apprentice and has not finished his term of apprenticeship in the said trade, shall be made free of the same trade; unless it be attested by the overseers for the time being, or by four persons of the said trade, that such person is able and sufficiently skilled to be made free of the same."

Cal. Let. Bk. G, 159.

[12] Memorials, 547. Leathersellers' ordinances of 1398. "That from henceforth no one shall set any man, child, or woman, to work in the same trade, if such person be not first bound apprentice, and enrolled in the trade; their wives and children only excepted."

Smith, English Gilds, 390. City of Worcester, Ordinances of 1467.

Hist. Charters and Constitutional Documents of the City of London, 186. City Ordinance of 1638. Widows may use trade without apprenticeship.

[13] Memorials, 217. Cal. Let. Bk. D, 99, 104, 115, 118, 130, 146, 151, 152, 159, 160, 162, 182.

Apprenticeship was also a qualification of admission into the franchise. A thirteenth century record mentions three methods of obtaining the franchise: "Sed sciendum est quod tribus modis adquiritur homini libertas civitatis: — Primo quod sit homo natus in civitate legitime ex patre; secondo quod homo sit apprenticius cum libero homine per septem annos et non minus, tertio quod homo mutuat suam libertatem̃ coram majore aliis aldermanis cum camerario civitatis."[14] All three methods — birth, apprenticeship, and redemption — constituted the practice for several centuries. A London ordinance of 1368 states that "there were only three ways whereby the said franchise could be obtained, viz., by birth, apprenticeship, or by presentment of some mistery before the Mayor, Aldermen, and Chamberlain."[15] A later ordinance of 1432 decrees "that fro this day forward no man be admitted in to the saide Fraunchise but he be born or made apprentice or officer with ynne the Citee."[16] Freedom "bi birth or apprenticialitie" became the most approved practice.[17] The custom of obtaining the franchise by redemption was in vogue, but was strongly discountenanced; a London ordinance of December 10, 1434 orders "the Aldermen to cause a certain number of men freemen of the City either by birth or apprenticeship, *and not by redemption*, to be elected members of the Common Council."[18] Indeed, the practice of obtaining the freedom of the City by redemption became so lax that an ordinance was passed by the Common Council to bring it within bounds.[19]

In this matter, as in others, the gilds followed the general practice that had been established by law; after all their regulations were but part of the common laws of the

---

[14] Chronicle of Edward I and Edward II, Vol. I, 85.
[15] Cal. Let. Bk. G, 179.
[16] Cal. Let. Bk. K, 161.
[17] *Ibid.*, 161.
[18] *Ibid.*, 190.
[19] *Ibid.*, 164.

country.[20] Upon completing his term the apprentice became a citizen and a member of the craft at the same time. Just as the city admitted into the franchise the sons of freemen, so the crafts admitted the sons of craftsmen without apprenticeship. In similar fashion the gilds disapproved the practice of redemption.[21]

Originally apprenticeship had been regulated only by private agreement between the master and the learner. Naturally there were abuses on each side; where public supervision had not yet become general covenants and oaths were frequently disregarded, and one or the other of the contracting parties suffered.[22] In order to insure fair play between members, and between masters and apprentices, the gilds came gradually to exercise the right of supervising the practice of apprenticeship. They realised, too, that not only must individual rights be protected, that fair conditions must be obtained for those who worked in the trade, but also that a tradition of skilled workmanship must be established and perpetuated in order to insure the production of wares of good quality. These objects could only be accomplished by mandatory legislation regulating the conditions of apprenticeship, and in this they were assisted by municipal authorities who confirmed the gild ordinances and gave them the force of law.

The earliest records concerning the regulation of apprenticeship reveal all the important characteristics of later practice. From the first craftsmen were forbidden by municipal legislation to take more apprentices than they were able to support and teach.[23] In some of the craft ordinances the same

[20] Liber Albus, 157, 272; Memorials, 282.

Memorials, 241. London Pewterers, 1348: "No one shall receive an apprentice against the usages of the City."

Coventry insisted that no crafts make laws except with the consent of the Mayor. City ordinances of 1421, 1475, 1515, in Coventry Leet Book, 29, 419, 645.

[21] Cal. Let. Bk. I, 63.

[22] Cal. Let. Bk. H, 34.   As early as 1376 a Scrivener is imprisoned for making a false indenture of apprenticeship with a boy.

Cal. Let. Bk. I, 215.

[23] Liber Albus, I, 383.   "Et que nulle desormes ne preigne apprentice plus qe deux ou trois a plus forsques sicomes il est de poiar de eux sustenir."

idea shows itself, that the taking of apprentices ought to depend altogether on the ability of the master "to keep, inform, and teach" them.[24] In the fifteenth century the rules become more definite in regard to limiting the number of apprentices each master might take. Thus, in 1466, the Tailors of Exeter limit the craftsmen to one apprentice.[25] In the Hull Weavers' Composition of 1490 we read: "Item, it is agreyd that non of that occupacon shall take and kepe bot two apprentises."[26] A similar requirement appears in the Coventry Cappers' Ordinances of 1496.[27] The Bricklayers of Hull, in their ordinances of 1598, also limit the master to two apprentices, but add the requirement that an interval of four years must elapse between the enrollment of each.[28] The custom had become pretty well established by this time, and the ordinances of the next century merely repeat the terms of earlier legislation.[29]

Liber Custumarum, 81. Articles of the Saddlers and Joiners of London, 1308: "Et qe nul fuster ne receyve aprentiz, si le seignour ne soit fraunk homme de la citee, et quil de soit de poiar de li sustenir a parfaire sez covenauntz."

[24] Memorials, 278.

[25] Smith, Eng. Gilds, 315–16. "Also hyt ys ordeyned, by the M. and Wardons and all the hole crafte, that fro hense-forthe no man of the said crafte shall hold but 3 seruauntes, and oo pryntes at the most, wt-owte lesanse of the M. and Wardonsse for the tyme beyng, apon payne of xlti. s."

See Clothworkers' Court Book, for 1537–1639, reprinted in Geo. Unwin, Industrial Organization in the 16th and 17th Centuries, 230. Master permitted to have but one apprentice.

[26] J. M. Lambert, Two Thousand Years of Gild Life, 206.

Cal. Let. Bk. K, 200. Mayor and Aldermen grant petition of London Girdlers, 1435, that no man of the craft should have more than two apprentices.

Cal. Let. Bk. K, 376. Founders of London, 1481.

Cal. Let. Bk. L, 201. London Brewers, 1482.

[27] Coventry Leet Book, 573.

[28] Lambert, 278. "Item, that none of this brotherhoode shall have above twoe apprentices at once, and that the firste apprentice shall have served fower yeares of his tearme before the seconde be taken to serve as an apprentice, in paine of everie one doeinge to the contrarie, to paie for everie tyme so doing, 3s."

[29] Lambert, 234. Hull Tailors' Ordinances of 1617: "That none should take a second prentice till the first has served four years; nor should take a third till the second had served five years."

Ibid., 313. Hull Cobblers' Ordinances of 1680: "And further is statuted, ordered and agreed upon that no free brother of the same trade shall take or en-

All the crafts required an entry-fee to be paid by the apprentice upon enrollment, and an exit-fee when he had served his term. The exit-fee signalised the admission of the apprentice into craft membership as a master and as a freeman of the City. The London Lorimers, mentioned above,[30] required in 1261 an entrance fee of 30 shillings, the Tailors of Lincoln, in 1328, required 2 shillings.[31] Perhaps the most common fee for both entry and exit during the fourteenth century was 2s. 6d. This seems to have been the established fee during the years 1309–1313 for the crafts of London.[32] We may reasonably assume, therefore, that this was the generally accepted practice as far as London was concerned, and that it was established by municipal legislation. During the fifteenth, sixteenth, and seventeenth centuries there was no uniformity of practice in this matter; the amounts varied from 4d. to £2.[33] This

tertaine a Second Apprentice untill the first Apprentice hath served as an Apprentice for the space of four yeares."

Ibid., 296. Hull Coopers' Ordinances of 1681: "Item it is ordered that noe Cooper ffree of this Companic shall kepe above two apprentices att once, upon paine to forfeit and pay for every such offence to the use of the said Company for every weeke herein offending, 10s."

[30] Page 1.

[31] Smith, Eng. Gilds, 183. In 1328 the Lincoln Tailors incorporated in their ordinances the rule that "If any master of the gild takes any one to live with him as an apprentice, in order to learn the work of the Tailor's craft, the apprentice shall pay two shillings to the gild."

Beverley Town Doc., 125. Beverley Butchers, 1365: "at his entre iis."

Manuscripts of Beverley, 92. Beverley Shoemakers: 20d.

[32] Upon examining some 415 records concerning apprenticeship during the years 1309–1313 (Cal. Let. Bk. D, 96–179), I found the phrase "for his ingress 2s. 6d.," used 244 times; and the phrase "for his exit, 2s. 6d.," used 75 times. This uniform fee was adopted by the following fifty crafts or trades, which represent fairly well the field of industrial occupation at that time: Apothecary, Barber, Blader, Boatman, Braeler, Bucklemaker, Bureller, Butcher, Buttermonger, Capper, Chandler, Chaucer, Cheesemaker, Cooper, Corder, Cordwainer, Cornmonger, Currier, Draper, Fishmonger, Fruiter, Fripperer, Fuster, Girdler, Glover, Goldsmith, Haberdasher, Hatter, Haymonger, Hosier, Ironmonger, Joiner, Knifemaker, Mercer, Ointer, Painter, Pepperer, Plumber, Potter, Pouchmaker, Saddler, Salter, Sealmaker, Shearman, Skinner, Tanner, Taverner, Vintner, Woodmonger, Woolmonger.

[33] On March 2, 1443, the London Common Council decreed that "in order to

requirement, like the ordinances directly concerned with the limitation of apprentices, served not only to keep down their number, and hence promote efficient trade training — one of the primary objects of gild regulation — but also protected adult workmen from the competition of juvenile labor.[34] Furthermore, it operated to reduce the number of those who attained the mastership, and thereby to diminish the competition of adult craftsmen with each other.

Apprentices were obliged by municipal legislation to enrol within the first year of their term. This regulation appeared very early [35] in the history of English apprenticeship, and was the authority for a long established custom. The gilds repeated it in their own ordinances.[36] Enrollment was a public matter; the apprentice appeared,[37] or was brought,[38]

---

relieve the increasing debts of the Chamber, the fees for enrolment of apprentices should for the next four years be doubled; viz., for entrances 5s., and the exits of the same 7s." Cal. Let. Bk. K, 292.

Beverley Town Docs., 103, 116; Manuscripts of Beverley, 97, 100; Coventry Leet Book, 641, 645.

[34] Cal. Let. Bk. K, 200. London Girdlers, 1435, complain: "nowe adayes ther is so gret abondaunce of apprentices of the seid craft that many freemen of the same craft which have but small quantitee of goodes of ther owen and were wont to live by the werk that thei made to other men of the same craft may now have no werk wt in the seid craft but som of hem be come Waterberers and laborers."

[35] As early as 1275. See page 2.

Cal. Let. Bk. H, 391. City ordinance of 1392.

Cal. Let. Bk. I, 38. City ordinance of 1404.

Ibid., 134. City ordinance of 1414.

Liber , Albus I, 655.

[36] Liber Custumarum, 81. Articles of the Saddlers and Joiners of London, 1308: "et qil le face enrouler en la Chaumbre de la Gihale, dedenz le primer an, sur la peyne qe appent."

Memorials, 258. Ordinances of London Furbishers, 1350.

[37] Cal. Let. Bk. D, 97. "Sept. 29, 1309: The same day John Whitlock . . . came before the Chamberlain and acknowledged himself apprentice of Geoffrey de Sterteford, glover, for a term of seven years from Michaelmas, 2s. 6d."

Ibid., 122. "July 11, 1310: The same day Richard . . . came before the Aldermen and Chamberlain, and acknowledged himself apprentice to John de Porkle, painter, for a term of six years."

Ibid., 144. "May 12, 1311, Godfrey . . . came before the aforesaid Mayor and Aldermen."

[38] Cal. Let. Bk. D, 66. "Mar. 16, 1310: Richard le Keu, chaloner, made

before the master of the craft and also before the mayor, or aldermen, or city chamberlain, and acknowledged himself indentured to a certain master craftsman. This acknowledgement, and the terms of the indenture or contract between the master and the apprentice were then enrolled, and became a public record.[39] Upon completion of the term of service the apprentice again appeared before the municipal authorities, and sought admission to his craft. The "Book" or "paper of apprentices"[40] was then consulted, and if "good men of the ward testified that the said apprentice had faithfully served his said master as apprentice,"[41] and was "a good and trusty man and fit to carry on the said trade," the apprentice paid the exit-fee and became a full-fledged master. This requirement of a double enrollment, upon entry and exit, secured for the contracting parties a certain amount of protection from abuse.

By the middle of the fourteenth century most crafts had required apprenticeship as the necessary preliminary to

fine of half a mark that he had with him apprentices and did not cause them to be enrolled according to the custom of the city, and he was commanded to bring those apprentices for enrolment under penalty prescribed."

Smith, Eng. Gilds, 316. Tailors' Ordinances, 1466. "Also hit is ordeyned by the M. and Wardons and all the hole crafte, that euery persone of the sayd crafte that taketh aprentys, shall brynge hym before the M. and Wardons, and there to haue his Indenture in-rolled."

[29] See Oath of Freemen, 1275, page 2, note 3.

The London Ordinance of 1279 or 1280, mentioned on page 2, required the master and apprentice to enroll their covenant and term "enceste manere qe le seignour et le prentice en ceo qe il meinovere en le mister veignent a la Guyhalle et facent enroller le covenant et le terme." (Liber Albus, I, 383–84)

Liber Custumarum, 124. Ordinances of London Weavers, 1300: "et qe lour covenant soit reconu en Court."

Memorials, 241. London Pewterers, 1384.

Calendar of Letters, 164. 1369.

Coventry Leet Book, 561. Coventry required, in 1494, that the apprentice's name be "entred in a boke remaynyng with the seid Styward (Steward) as a Registre."

[40] Apparently each ward of the City of London kept a "Book" or "paper of apprentices." The reference appears 114 times for 23 wards, during the years 1275–1322 (Cal. Let. Bk. D, 96–179).

[41] Cal. Let. Bk. D, 106, 122, 124, 149, 150, 152, 154, 157, 161, 170, 178.

mastership. It had become a fixed custom at this time to require the master and apprentice to draw up an indenture or covenant containing the articles of mutual agreement which defined their relationship to each other.[42] The usual term of service was seven years, although terms as short as two years and as long as sixteen appear frequently in the records.[43] Municipal and craft ordinances when they touched

[42] City records for the years 1309–13 mention frequently "a certain writing indented of his apprenticeship," and "a certain writing indented made between them." (Cal. Let. Bk. D, 96–179)

A letter, dated 1351, contains "by indentures between them made according to the custom of the City of London." (Calendar of Letters, 11)

Cal. Let. Bk. K, 337. Ordinances of the London Cordwainers, confirmed by the Mayor and Aldermen, April 6, 1451: "that it may be ordeigned enact and enrolled in the forsaid Chaumber of Guyldhall that no manere persone nowe beyng enfrauncheised in the said craft ne which hereafter shall be from hens forthe resceive ne take eny manere persone to teche and enforme him in the same craft, but that he take him as an apprentice by a peyre of indentures of apprentishode to be made betwene the maister and every suche persone after the rule and ordinance this Citee."

The Ordinances of the City of Worcester, Sept. 14, 1467, required "that ther be endenturs made bitwen hem for the seid term as the law requirith." (Smith, Eng. Gilds, 390)

Lambert, 216. Hull Glovers, 1499.

[43] The following table based on records for the years 1309–1313 (Cal. Let. Bk. D, 96–179) shows the length of term, and the number of times each term appears:

Term	Appears in records	Term	Appears in records
2 years	3 times	10 years	44 times
3 "	3 "	11 "	6 "
4 "	2 "	12 "	13 "
5 "	3 "	13 "	1 "
6 "	12 "	14 "	6 "
7 "	138 "	15 "	1 "
8 "	64 "	16 "	1 "
9 "	17 "	"full term"	101 "

The Letter-Book before us records the apprenticeships of 415 boys to at least 50 different trades. 138 boys acknowledged themselves apprenticed for seven-year terms, one third of the number recorded. The expression "full term" appears 101 times. It is safe to say that the majority of these "full terms" were for seven years.

A letter dated Aug. 18, 1354, contains the following excerpt which represents the type of record that appears frequently: "bound apprentice according to the custom of the City of London, for a term of seven years." (Calendar of Letters, 65)

upon the proper term of apprenticeship, usually insisted upon its lasting at least seven years. This period was required by a London ordinance as early as 1279.[44] The ordinances of nearly all the crafts conformed to a common type which may be represented by the Weavers' Ordinances of 1300: "No weaver shall receive an apprentice for less than a term of seven years."[45] The Hatters in 1347,[46] the Braelers in 1355,[47] and the Masons[48] in the following year, passed by-laws enforcing a minimum term of seven years, "according to the usages of the City." Outside London this requirement appears as early as 1307, in the ordinances of the York Girdlers,[49] and as early as 1421, in the Coventry Barbers' Composition.[50] Again, we find the City of Worcester, in 1467, demanding a "fulle vii yere of prentishode."[51] Numerous records might be quoted to show how generally accepted this custom was until its final establishment by the Statute of Apprentices, 1562.[52]

For the purposes of this study chief interest attaches to the terms of the indenture or covenant between master and apprentice. Several early indentures of apprenticeship have been printed.[53] One of the earliest, dated 1291, contains most of the articles of later covenants, although its phraseology

[44] Page 2.

[45] Liber Custumarum, 124. "Et qe nul teler aprentiz ne receyve a meyns qe a terme de vii aunz."

[46] Memorials, 238.

[47] Memorials, 278.

[48] Memorials, 282.

Ibid., 439. Ordinances of London Cutlers, 1379.

Ibid., 354. London Haberdashers, 1371.

[49] York Memorandum Book, Vol. I, 181. "That na maister fra this tyme forth tak nane apprentice for less terme than vii yere."

[50] Coventry Leet Book, 225.

[51] Smith, Eng. Gilds, 390.

[52] Coventry Leet Book, 573. Coventry Cappers, 1496.

Lambert, 205. Hull Weavers, 1490; *Ibid.*, 216. Hull Glovers, 1499; etc.

[53] 1291, in Hudson and Tingey, The Records of the City of Norwich, Vol. I, 245; 1396, in Archæological Journal, XXIX (London, 1872), 184; 1414, in Hibbert, Influence and Development of English Gilds, 52; 1451, in Rogers, History of Agriculture and Prices, Vol. IV, 98; 1480, in Cunningham, English Industry.

does not conform to the type which is represented by two indentures of the years 1396,[54] and 1414. The latter are practically identical in form and content with the indentures of the present century. From them we learn that the apprentice bound himself to live with his master for a certain period of years, promised to serve him diligently, obey his "reasonable" commands, keep his secrets, protect him from injury "by others," abstain from such games as dice and cards, and the "haunting" of taverns, neither to commit fornication nor contract matrimony, and not to absent himself from his master's service without permission.[55] The master, on the other hand, promised to instruct the boy in his trade, and give him bed, board, and clothing.[56] This instruction must have been fairly skilled in character because the master himself had graduated from a similar course of training, and had proved his skill before the gild.[57] If the master did not fulfill his agreement in respect to instruction and maintenance, he was reported to the gild by inspectors or "Searchers," and subjected to a penalty. Apprentices were taken from masters financially unable to support them, and indentured to others in the same craft

[54] See Appendix A. Copy of 1396 indenture of apprenticeship.

[55] Hibbert, 52. Indenture of apprenticeship from the Mercers' Company's Records, 1414. "A servicio suo seipsum illicite non absentabit. Bona et catalla dicti Johannis absque ejus licentia nulli accomodabit. Tabernam, scortum, talos, aleas, et joca similia non frequentabit, in dispendium magistri sui. Fornicationem nec adulterium cum aliqua muliere de domo et familia dicti Johannis nullo modo committet, neque uxorem ducet, absque licentia magistri sui. Præcepta et mandata licita et racionabilia magistri sui ubique pro fideli posse ipsius Gulielmi, diligenter adimplebit et eisdem mandatis libenter obediet."

[56] Hudson and Tingey, I, 245. Indenture dated June 10, 1291. "eidem Johanni in omnibus prout decet humiliter fideliter competenter pro posse suo interim deseruiendo . . . et secreta sua que fueri ntconcelanda firmiter concelabit. . . . Et dictus Johannes per totum dictum tempus docebit dictum Hubertum officium suum quo utitur . . . Et idem Johannes vel eius assignatus per totum dictum tempus inueniet dicto Huberto cibos et potum vestimenta linea et calciamenta."

[57] In order to insure efficient training, the craft of Writers of Court-letter required in 1439 "That no one enfranchised of the craft, without special licence, shall occupy or hold open more than one shop, in order that he may watch his apprentices and examine all feates made by them." (Cal. Let. Bk. K, 235)

for the remainder of the original term. In some cases, and with the sanction of the gild, a master might sell some years of an apprentice's service to another master.[58] A new indenture was then made and recorded with the conditions of the transfer. In the event of the master's death the apprentice usually served the remainder of his term with the person to whom the indenture was bequeathed.[59] Gild and municipal authorities alike exercised a rigid supervision over both parties to the indenture, and insisted upon the fulfilment of all lawful agreements.[60]

It is evident that the relationship was not only that of master-craftsman to learner, but was also, essentially, that of father to son. The master was responsible for the moral welfare of the apprentice as well as for teaching him his trade. In cases of transgression and incorrigibility the master was permitted to administer the proper punishment, but if the apprentice was unduly punished he could appeal to and obtain redress from the craft and city authorities.[61]

[58] A letter dated Nov. 5, 1369 mentions "John Notekyn, whose term of apprenticeship had been sold," (Calendar of Letters, 170)

Cal. Let. Bk. D, 171.

[59] A letter dated 1351 contains the following: "The said John de Pateneye having lately died, had devised by will the remaining term of the said apprentice to Agnes his wife." (Calendar of Letters, 11)

A London will dated Aug. 6, 1428, reads: "I wil that the same Henri have all the termes comyng to me of Henry Clopton, myn other apprentice." (The Fifty Earliest English Wills, 78)

[60] Middlesex Records, II, 47. Court record dated Jan. 12, 1608, reads: "Ordered that Thomas Thomas an apprentice to John Stocke of Ratcliffe taylor shalbe discharged out of his master's service, and his indentures to be cancelled because John Stocke hath not maintayned him with sufficient apparell as an apprentice ought to have."

Ibid., III, 328. Nov. 5, 1663, master punished "for that he refuseth to teach him (the apprentice) his trade."

[61] Smith, Eng. Gilds, 322. The records of the Exeter Tailors contain the following: "Md., of a-warde y-made bi the maister and Wardons the 16th day of July, the yeere of the Reigne of Kyng Edward the 4th, the 21st (1480), bitwene William Peeke and John Lynch; for that the said William un-lawfully chasted hym, in brusyn of his arm and broke his hedd. And for that it was chuged, bi the said maister and wardons, that the said William Peeke shuld pay, for his leche craifte, 5s; and for his table, for a moneth 3s. 4d; and for amendis, 15s; and to craifte, 20d, for a fyne for his mysbehaueing aynst the craift."

Since the responsibility for his good behavior rested with the master, the boy's moral conduct was under constant supervision both inside and outside working hours. This was required by gild and city ordinances, and was made possible by the fact that he lived with his master.

So far only boy-apprenticeship has been considered. It may be pertinent, at this point, to mention the fact that girls were admitted into the crafts under the same conditions that regulated the practice for boys.[62] It is not an uncommon thing to find women and girls enrolled as members of crafts where one would least expect them, such as the founders,[63] barber-surgeons,[64] brewers,[65] carpenters,[66] wheelwrights,[67] and clockmakers.[68]

Let us turn now from the foregoing brief treatment of apprenticeship as a local custom, to its establishment as a national institution. Until 1562 apprenticeship had been a general practice throughout England, but its regulation had differed in different localities. In that year the Statute of Artificers transformed it into a national system which op-

---

Middlesex Records, III, 328. Master punished by town authorities, 1663, for administering "unlawful correction."

[62] Cal. Let. Bk. E, 200. A London record of June 4, 1335, mentions "the said Isabella and for teaching her a trade as an apprentice."

Cal. Let. Bk. H, 391. London ordinance, 1392, "ordained that no man or woman take a male or female apprentice unless enrolled within the first year of their term."

Cal. Let. Bk. I, 134. London ordinance of 1414.

Burough Customs, 230. "Law of Apprentices, London, 1419: Married women who practice certain crafts in the city, may take girls as their apprentices, and these apprentices shall be bound by indentures."

Ricart, Kalendar, 102. Girl-apprentices, 1479.

Cal. Let. Bk. L, 186. Articles of Wiredrawers, 1481, allow admission of wives, sons, daughters without apprenticeship.

Cal. Let. Bk. K, 87, 104–05.

[63] Stahlschmidt, Surrey Bells and London Bell-Founders, 51, 54.

[64] Young, Annals of the Barber-Surgeons, 260.

[65] Unwin, Gilds of London, 191.

[66] Jupp, Carpenters, 161.

[67] Scott, Wheelwrights, 16.

[68] Overall, Clockmakers, 155.

Coventry Leet Book, 271, 555, 652, 658, 673.

erated everywhere in the same manner. By this Act the whole gild system was remodeled, and trade regulation was made national instead of local. The reasons for drawing up the Act are given in the preamble: first, the need of a readjustment of the standard of wages; second, the necessity of codifying the numerous laws on the employment of servants and apprentices.[69] Many of these were out of date, while others were contradictory. Here apprenticeship was regulated by custom, here by charter, and there left undetermined. In one place a certain period of service was exacted, in another place a different period. The need for reform and the better regulation of industry had been felt for some time, and finally the leaders of the day saw that the remedy lay in a general and consolidating statute. This statute not only embodied the experience derived from earlier measures, but also incorporated everything worth taking in the ordinances of the gilds, and made general certain conditions of industry which the gilds had been the first distinctly to formulate.

We are here concerned with the statute only so far as it affects the practice of apprenticeship. The principal regulations are the following:

Every person being a householder and 24 years old at least, and exercising any art, mystery or manual occupation, may . . . retain the son of any freeman not occupying husbandry nor being a labourer, to be bound

[69] Select Statutes, 45. "Although there remain in force presently a great number of statutes concerning apprentices, servants and labourers, as well in husbandry as in divers other . . . occupations, yet partly for the imperfection and contrariety . . . . in sundry of the said laws, and for the variety and number of them . . . the said laws cannot conveniently without the greatest grief and burden of the poor labourer and hired man be put into execution . . . so if the substance of as many of the said laws as are meet to be continued shall be digested and reduced into one sole law and Statute, and in the same an uniform Order prescribed and limited concerning the wages and other Orders for Apprentices, Servants and Labourers, there is good hope that it will come to pass, that the same law should banish Idleness, advance Husbandry, and yield unto the hired person, both in time of Scarcity and in time of Plenty, a convenient Proportion of Wages."

This Act repealed 34 statutes since Edward III so far as they concerned the hiring, keeping, wages, etc., of servants, labourers, and apprentices.

as an apprentice after the custom and order of the city of London for 7 years at the least, so as the term of such apprentice do not expire afore such apprentice shall be of the age of 24 years at the least.[70]

Every person that shall have three apprentices in any of the said crafts of clothmaker, fuller, shearman, weaver, tailor, or shoemaker shall keep one journeyman, and for every other apprentice above the number of the said three apprentices one other journeyman, upon pain of every default therein £10.[71]

If any person shall be required by any householder having half a ploughland at the least in tillage to be an apprentice and to serve in husbandry or in any other kind of art before expressed and shall refuse so to do, then upon complaint of such householder made to one Justice of Peace in the county wherein such refusal is made, or to the mayor, bailiffs or head officer . . . they shall have full power to send for the same person so refusing; and if the said Justice or head officer shall think the said person meet to serve as an apprentice in that art . . . the said Justice or head officer shall have power . . . to commit him unto ward, there to remain until he will be bounden to serve . . . and if any such master shall evil treat his apprentice . . . or if the apprentice do not his duty to his master, then the said master or apprentice being grieved shall repair to one Justice of the Peace in the said county . . . who shall . . . take such order and direction between the said master and his apprentice as the equity of the case shall require.[72]

The apprenticeship clauses quoted above were, it seems, really intended to check departure from a rule which had become an established custom, and had been recognised and enforced by the gilds and local authorities. Any substantial householder might take a boy to serve as an apprentice in husbandry till his twenty-first or twenty-fourth year "as the parties can agree." For manufacturing industry the duration of apprenticeship was fixed; the old minimum of seven years service was required for all artisans, with the proviso added by the statute: "so as the term of such apprentice do not expire afore such apprentice shall be of the age of twenty-four years at the least."[73] Apparently

---

[70] Select Statutes, 50. 5 Eliz. c. 4. Sect. XIX.

[71] Select Statutes, 52. Sect. XXVI.

[72] Select Statutes, 52. Sect. XXVIII.

[73] Craft ordinances subsequent to 1562 insist upon the seven-year term, or "until 24 years of age."

the objects were: to provide adequate trade training and to lessen unemployment by preventing employers from going outside the ranks of trained men. If a boy, not legally exempted, refused to serve "in husbandry or in any other kind of art," he was brought before a Justice of the Peace, and committed "unto ward there to remain until he will be bounden to serve." As in earlier gild practice apprentices must be bound by indenture, and the terms of the agreement enrolled;[74] and if either master or apprentice violated any of the articles of the indenture, the injured person could secure redress in a public court, at the hands of a Justice of the Peace or a "head officer." Furthermore, the proportion of apprentices to journeymen was settled; in a number of trades, presumably those which showed a tendency for the apprenticeship system to be perverted into a means for obtaining cheap labor, every master who

---

Lambert, 207. Hull Weavers' ordinances of 1564.

Beverley Manuscripts, 83. Beverley Mercers, 1582: "7 years according to the Statute."

Lambert, 252. Hull Joiners, 1598.

Ibid., 286. Hull Coopers, 1598.

Ibid., 278. Hull Bricklayers, 1599.

Ibid., 234. Hull Tailors, 1617: "Each apprentice should be twenty-four years old before his apprenticeship should expire."

Ibid., 323. Hull Cordwainers, 1624: "24 yeares according to the Statute."

Ibid., 254. Hull Joiners, 1629.

Historical Charters, 189. London Ordinance of 1638.

Lambert, 174. Hull Merchants, 1649.

Ibid., 210. Hull Weavers, 1673.

Ibid., 244. Hull Tailors, 1680: "Seven years according to the Statute."

Smith, Eng. Gilds, 209. London Joiners, 1682.

Lambert, 363. Hull Barbers, 1714.

[74] Lambert, 244. Hull Tailors, 1680: "Indentures inrolled as well in the Town's book as in the Company's book . . . according to the Statute."

Ibid., 313. Hull Cobblers, 1680: "in the Towne's booke."

Ibid., 296. Hull Coopers, 1681: "enrolled in the Companie's booke . . . and in the ye townis Booke of Enrolments within one yeare."

Ibid., 346. Hull Shipwrights, 1682: "at the Town's Hall."

Ibid., 267, 287. In 1580 the following crafts of Hull agreed to take no apprentices without the consent of the Mayor and Aldermen: goldsmiths, smiths, pewterers, plumbers, glaziers, painters, cutlers, musicians, coopers, stationers, bookbinders, basketmakers.

had more than three apprentices was compelled to employ one journeyman for every extra apprentice. The security which this requirement gave against overstocking with apprentices also facilitated their receiving proper instruction.

The Poor Law of 1601 gave the public authorities additional powers with regard to apprenticeship. At the time when this Act was passed the relief of the poor was one of the most pressing questions of the day. The numbers and misery of the poor and unemployed had been increasing for centuries. The dissolution of the monasteries, the inclosure evils which attended the transition from husbandry to grazing, the fall in the demand for labor, successive debasements of the coinage, the rise of prices — all combined to create a situation of extreme distress among the lower classes. A natural consequence was that vagabondage, idleness, and poverty increased, and constituted a very real problem. In previous reigns numerous repressive statutes, imposing severe penalties upon the "sturdy beggar," had been tried out and proved ineffective. Perhaps the most successful remedy for this condition of widespread distress was that of compulsory apprenticeship as required by the Statute of 1562. The legislators of Elizabeth had before them the experiments of Henry VIII and Edward VI, and their convictions concerning these earlier attempts at remedial legislation were verified by the improvement which followed the passage of the Statute of Apprentices. It was, then, only natural that in 1601 they should see in apprenticeship a partial solution of the problem of pauperism, and in that year was enacted the Poor Law which consolidated previous Acts into one comprehensive measure designed to "provide work for those who could work, relief for those who could not, and punishment for those who would not." [75]

As with the Act of 1562, our chief interest in the Poor Law of 1601 is in the sections that are concerned with apprenticeship. In this connection the following are important:

[75] Cunningham, The Growth of English Industry and Commerce, II, 61.

Be it enacted . . . that the church-wardens of every parish, and four three or two substantial householders there, as shall be thought meet, having respect to the proportion and greatness of the same parish and parishes, to be nominated yearly . . . under the hand and seal of two or more justices of the peace in the same county . . . shall be called overseers of the poor of the same parish: and they . . . shall take order from time to time, by and with the consent of two or more justices of the peace as is aforesaid for setting to work such children of all those whose parents shall not by the said church-wardens and overseers, or the greater part of them, be thought able to keep and maintain their children. . . .

And be it further enacted that it shall be lawful for the said church wardens and overseers, or the greater part of them, by the assent of any two justices of the peace aforesaid, to bind any such children, as aforesaid, to be apprentices, where they shall see convenient, till such man-child shall come to the age of four and twenty years and such woman-child to the age of one and twenty years, or the time of her marriage; the same to be effectual to all purposes, as if such child were of full age, and by indenture or covenant bound him or herself.[76]

This Act made it lawful for church-wardens and overseers to apprentice all poor-children, males until twenty-four years of age, and females until twenty-one or marriage. In 1767 (7 Geo. III. c. 39) the term for parish-apprentices was revised to read: "for seven years only or until the age of twenty-one years," and in 1778 (18 Geo. III. c. 47) a general Act declared that no apprentice should be bound after twenty-one years of age. It is important to note at this point that Poor Law apprenticeship differed from industrial apprenticeship, in that its primary object was not so much to teach the apprentice a trade as to "bind him out" to a person who would maintain him. It was the duty of the overseers and church-wardens to provide him with "bed, board and clothing," and a guardian. Although technical instruction was not included, it so happened that a great many "pauper apprentices" received such training from masters who were engaged in industrial pursuits. In accordance with the earlier custom an indenture was required to be drawn up setting forth the terms under which the apprentice served, and this agreement was publicly recorded.

[76] Select Statutes, 103.

The terms of the indenture were similar to those for the industrial apprentices; the phraseology, however, differed slightly. In this case the overseers were parties to the contract, they "put out" or "bound" poor-children, and their names appeared in the indenture. Furthermore, all apprenticing or binding, to be legal, must be done with consent of two Justices of the Peace, and to these officers were referred all complaints by the contracting parties.

In this study we are not especially interested in the enforcement of the Acts of 1562 and 1601, but rather in the practice which they defined and established. The records show that these laws were rather irregularly administered. In some instances the apprenticeship clauses of the Statute of Apprentices were disregarded. We know also that the Poor Law of 1601 did not adequately provide for the physical well-being of parish-apprentices; many cases of abuse are recorded. But they did give legal authority to a practice which was continued in England until the early 19th century. In 1814 the apprenticeship clauses of the Statute of Apprentices were repealed, and in 1834 the Poor Law Amendment Act was passed. With the enactment of these Statutes the old apprenticeship system came to an end.

In the succeeding chapters an attempt will be made to show the reproduction and continuation of the apprenticeship system in the English colonies of New England and New York. Several important modifications of the old system were made in colonial practice; some features disappeared, others more significant for the history of American colonial education were added. The emphasis throughout will be upon the educational aspects of this practice.

CHAPTER II

THE PRACTICE OF APPRENTICESHIP IN THE NEW PLYMOUTH AND MASSACHUSETTS BAY COLONIES

In the English colonies in America the practice of apprenticeship enjoyed a geographical distribution as widespread as the colonies themselves. The earliest settlers brought with them the custom and tradition of the mother-country, and continued those usages which they found expedient to their needs. In some instances, as we shall see, the English practice was modified to suit conditions, and it came soon to assume a new significance in the life of the time. Indeed, the apprenticeship system played a far more important part in colonial life than we have been accustomed to ascribe to it; its significance has not been sufficiently emphasized. Not only was apprenticeship of fundamental social and economic importance, as in England, but it was the most fundamental educational institution of the period.

There were two kinds or classes of child-apprenticeship in the American colonies: voluntary, and compulsory, or forced.[1] The voluntary apprentice bound himself "by his own free will and consent" to a master in order to learn a trade. The second class of apprentices comprises those who were bound out by colony or town authorities in accordance with the practice established by the Statute of Artificers and the Poor Law of 1601. The act of 1562, as such, was not continued in the New England and New York colonies; at least they did not interpret literally, and enforce the provision which permitted "any householder having half a ploughland at the least in tillage" to require "any person

---

[1] This study is not concerned with adult apprentices, redemptioners, and indented servants.

to be an apprentice to serve in husbandry or in any other kind of art before expressed." The general principles, and procedure, however, were adopted in most cases without direct action by colonial legislatures. All children "not having estates otherwise to maintain themselves" were obliged to engage in some form of useful occupation, and apprenticeship, as in England, was the customary method of entering a trade. The boy of average means chose the calling he desired to follow, or his parent or guardian chose it for him, and apprenticed himself to a master who could give the necessary instruction. Poor-children were bound out by town officials to masters who could provide maintenance as required by the Law of 1601. Later, as we shall see, when colony and town legislation turned its attention to the care of poor-apprentices, masters were obliged to give them trade-training and education.

From the beginning, in New England, we find evidence of the continuance of an important aspect of the English practice, i.e., public enrollment of indentures. When a master took an apprentice he was obliged, with the apprentice, to subscribe to a mutual covenant or indenture before reliable witnesses. This document, to be legal, must then be registered or recorded with the town authorities. As a public record, it assured both parties a large amount of protection from violation of the articles of their agreement. That this requirement was generally observed is evident from the fact that most of the records of apprenticeship are contained in court, and town-meeting minutes.[2] There occurred but few instances of non-compliance with this regulation. Lechford, in 1639, entered in his diary a case of violation of covenant, and of the enrollment requirement:

Dermondt Matthew did bind Teg Matthew his sonne a child of 9 yeares old apprentice to the said George Strange for ten yeares from the said 9th of May (1639) with Covenant to keepe him two yeares at school.

[2] These records follow such headings as: "At a meeting"; "At a General Court"; "At a Court before the Governor & Assistants"; "Things done by the Govr & Cowncell."

. . . But the said George Strange hath without the consent of the said Dermondt sold the said Tegg to one Mr. Browne of Salem to his the said Dermondts great grief of heart & *contrary to the said Covenant.* And whereas the said Dermondt being an illitered man & trusting upon the faire promises of the said George Strange that he would ever use him well & shew him his Indentures as often as he would now the said Dermondt having no chest nor box to put the said Indentures in they were rotted & spoiled in his pocket before he was aware. Notwithstanding the said George Strange refuseth to let the said Dermondt or his Friends see the Indentures. Therefore the said *Dermondt Matthew humbly prayeth the Court that the said Indentures may be shewed to the Court by the said George Strange & that they may be recorded.*[3]

To remind the inhabitants of the English regulation, and to prevent an increase of such violations, Boston, in 1660, passed the following law:

All indentures made between any master and servant shall bee brought in and enrolled in the Town's Records within one month after the contract made, on penalty of ten shillings be paid by the master att the time of the Apprentices being made free.[4]

At the expiration of the term of service the master appeared again "Att a meeting" of the town officials, and "acknowledged . . . his saruant hath serued his time of Aprentiship according to his Endenturs."[5] Completions, as well as enrollments, must be entered in the town records. If the apprentice had "well and truly" served his master,

[3] Lechford's Note Book, 251.
Records and Files of the Quarterly Courts of Essex County, III, 366.

[4] Boston Records, II, 157
Occasional records, of which the following is a type, refer to this regulation: "20.1.61. Att a meeting of Hezekiah Usher, Petter Olliver . . . Christopher Pickett with the Consent of ye Selectmen, put forth his daughter Mary Pickett an apprentice for 14 yeares and 4 monthes to Griffine Craft of Roxberry as appears by indenture baring date the 18 March 61 *wich Indenture is Kept amongst the Town Records.*" (Boston Records, VII, 6)

Boston Records, VII, 67. A Boston order of 1672 directs parents to "make returne of the names of Mastrs & Children soe put out to seruice, with their Indentures to the Selectmen at their nexte monethly Meeting."

Watertown Records, I, 129. "A metting of the selectmen . . . the 27th of march 1677 . . . . and Simon Stone to make agrement betwene him and the boy *and to record it in the town booke.*"

[5] Boston Records, VII, 28. Record dated 30:8:65.

he was permitted to follow his calling or trade,[6] but "if any have bene unfaithful negligent, or unprofitable in their service, notwithstanding the good usage of their maisters, they shall not be dismissed till they have made satisfaction according to the Judgment of Authoritie."[7] The town insisted upon its artisans serving a successful apprenticeship before setting up in their respective trades.

The term of service, in accordance with the custom and law of the mother-country, must not be completed until the apprentice had arrived at the age of twenty-one, and had served at least seven years. Girl-apprentices were required to serve until eighteen years of age, or until they were married.[8] As in England, seven years constituted the prescribed term, and, although colonial legislation had not yet touched on the matter, most of the records indicate that this regulation was observed.[9] The seven-year term is mentioned in the records of the earliest settlers of Boston: from the minutes of "a Court holden att Boston, July 26th, 1631," we learn that "Lucy Smith is bound an apprentice with Roger Ludlow for 7 yeares."[10] It is not unusual, however, to find instances in which this requirement was violated. Terms as short as four, five, and six years appear

[6] Boston Records, II, 137. "At a meting . . . 29th of 4th 1657. John Clow having served an Apprenticeship hath Liberty to follow his Calling in this Town."

[7] Old South Leaflets, Vol. 7, No. 164. The Liberties of the Massachusetts Collonie in New England, Dec. 1641.

[8] The English custom required that girls serve until twenty years of age. An instance in which this requirement was observed occurs in the minutes of "a Court, holden att Newe Towne, March 3, 1634," at which a girl is apprenticed "till she attaine the age of twenty yeares." (Records of the Governor and Colony of Mass. Bay in New England, Vol. I, 134) A Salem town meeting of 1648, however, ordered "the mayde" to be apprenticed "till the age of 18 years." (Felt, Annals of Salem, II, 397) Later "18 years of age" is the limit established by law. (New Plymouth, 1671, Mass. Bay, 1692, *et seq.*)

[9] Recs. Col. New Plymouth, I, 12, 15, 16, 23, 29, 31, 35, 36, 37, 43, 46, 82, 110, 128. Records for the years 1633–45, containing terms of 7 years or above.

Lechford, 151, 153, 175, 251, 362, 437. Records for 1638–41.

Felt, Annals of Salem, II, 396. Date 1644.

Records and Files, I, 113, 132, 163, 201, 231; II, 295, 311; III, 117, 309; IV, 54. Records of 1647–66.

[10] Mass. Bay Records, I, 90.

occasionally in the records of Massachusetts Bay and New Plymouth.[11] But the colonists soon realized that if this practice were allowed to continue, the cardinal principle of apprenticeship — the training of skilled artisans — would be perverted. New legislation was necessary, therefore, to reemphasize and enforce this aspect of the English practice. In 1660 Boston passed the following very definitive law regulating the term of apprenticeship:

> 20th, 6th mo., 1660.   Att a Towne's meeting . . .
>
> Whereas itt is found by sad experience that youthes of this town, beinge put forth Apprentices to severall manufactures and sciences, but for 3 or 4 yeares time, contrary to the Customes of all well governed places, whence they are uncapable of being Artists in their trades, beside their unmeetness att the expiration of their Apprenticeship to take charge of others for government and manuall instruction in their occupations which, if not timely amended, threatens the welfare of this Town.
>
> It is therefore ordered that no person shall henceforth open a shop in this Town, nor occupy any manufacture or science, till hee hath compleated 21 years of age, nor except hee hath served seven yeares Apprenticeship, by testimony under the hands of sufficient witnesses. And that all Indentures made between any master and servant shall bee brought in and enrolled in the Towne's Records within one month after the contract made, on penalty of ten shillings be paid by the master att the time of the Apprentices being made free.[12]

All subsequent apprenticeship legislation repeats the seven-year requirement, and the records show that it was generally complied with,[13] "7 yeares seruice being so much as ye

[11] Mass. Bay Records, 198–99.

Lechford, 162, 203, 235, 363.

Recs. Col. New Plymouth, I, 15–16, 24, 64, 110.

[12] Boston Records, II, 157.

Boston Records, VII, 39. "24:12:1667: Where as James Hull hath sett up the trade of Cooper, Haueing not serued aprentiship according to Towne order, is forbidden to occupye the said trade; as to keping open shop, one the forfeiture of 10s p. month."

[13] Boston Records, VII, 6, 37. Dates 1661, 1667.

York Deeds, Book I, Folio 115; Book II, Folios 62, 129, 141; Book III, Folios 12, 73. Dates 1661–79.

New Hampshire Hist. Soc. Coll., VIII, 287. Date 1676.

Sewall's Diary, I, 345. Date 1691.

practice of old England, & thought meet in this place.''[14]

An interesting instance of enforcement of the 1660 law reveals the colonial attitude toward exemptions from the apprenticeship requirement.

24: 12: 1667. Att a meeting of Mr. Petter Oliuer, Hezekiah Usher, Capt. James Oliuer, Capt. Th. Lake, Joshua Scottow, Edward Ranceford, & John Hull.

Upon complaint by the Coopers that John Farnum Senior, doth imploy his sonne in order to the setting up the trade of a Cooper without serueing 7 yeares apprentize to the said trade, contrary to a Town order, The Selectmen haue forbidden John Farnum Senior, to permitt his sonne to sett up the trade of a Cooper, Unless he serue the prentiship of 7 yeares one penalty of 10s p. month.[15]

It is probable that John Farnum senior had assumed that the early custom was still recognised of admitting sons into the craft without apprenticeship. But this practice was not continued; the "Town order" mentioned emphatically forbade anyone to engage in trade "except hee hath served seven yeares Apprenticeship." This principle obtained not only in the Massachusetts Bay colony, but it was operative in all the American colonies.

There were no craft organisations as such in the colonies, but occasionally those engaged in a particular trade came together for the purpose of defining methods of procedure which would benefit all artisans. In the case quoted in the preceding paragraph the coopers came before the town officials to demand the enforcement of a regulation which protected their reputation for skilled workmanship. Town and colony authorities took care of all matters pertaining to trade regulation.

To understand the relationship that existed between master and apprentice it is necessary to examine the indenture. The earliest references to apprenticeship in the New Plymouth

New England Hist. and Geneal. Register, Vol. 34, 311; Vol. 33, 18. Dates 1747, 1751.

Hist. Coll. Essex Institute, II, 86. Date 1757.

[14] Records and Files, II, 295. Salem, June 25, 1661.

[15] Boston Records, VII, 39.

and Massachusetts Bay colonies are contained in court records, and are, therefore, abbreviated. Hence, they are not complete enough for our purposes. Two such records will suffice to show the type.

A Court, holden att Boston, July 3, 1632.

John Smith is bound apprentice to Mr. John Wilson for five yeares from this court, dureing wch tearme Mr. Wilson is to finde the said John Smyth meate, drinke, and appel.[16]

From this we learn only that the apprentice was bound for five years, and that the master was to provide "meate, drinke, and appel." Additional information concerning the mutual obligations of master and apprentice is given in the record of "A Generall Court" of New Plymouth, held Jan. 6, 1633:

Sam Jenny the sonne of John Jenny, by the consent of the said John, hat bound himselfe apprentise to Kanelm Wynslow, of Plymouth, joyner for the full terme of fowr yeares, during wch time the said Samuel shall doe faithful service, as becometh an apprentise, to the said Kanelm. Also the said Kanelm shall . . . doe his best to instruct him in his trade, and at the end of his tyme shall dowble appel the said Samuel.[17]

Here the apprentice promised to "doe faithful service," and the master agreed to "doe his best to instruct him in his trade," and give him double apparel at the end of his service.

I was unable to secure a complete Massachusetts Bay indenture of an earlier date than 1676. The following covenant of the district of New Hampshire completes the more or less fragmentary description given by the records quoted above, and presents a detailed account of the relationship under consideration:

[16] Mass. Bay Records, I, 98.

Ibid., I, 90, 99, 134.

[17] Recs. Col. New Plymouth, I, 24.

Ibid., I, 15. July 23, 1633: "the trade of carpentry, wherein the said Richard sufficiently to instruct and teach him."

Ibid., I, 16. Aug. 15, 1633: "the said William promising to instruct and teach him the said trade of nayling, & at the end of his time to giue him only two sutes of apparell."

This Indenture witnesseth that I, Nathan Knight, sometime of Black point, with the consent of my father-in-law, Harry Brooken, and Elend. his wife, have put myself apprentice to Samuel Whidden, of Portsmouth, in the county of Portsmouth, mason, and bound after the manner of an apprentice with him, to serve and abide the full space and term of twelve years and five months, thence next following, to be full, complete and ended; during which time the said apprentice his said master faithfully shall serve, his lawful secrets shall keep, and commands shall gladly do, damage unto his said master he shall not do, nor see to be done of others, but to the best of his power shall give timely notice thereof to his said master. Fornication he shall not commit, nor contract matrimony within the said time. The goods of his said master, he shall not spend or lend. He shall not play cards, or dice, or any other unlawful game, whereby his said master may have damage in his own goods, or others, taverns, he shall not haunt, nor from his master's business absent himself by day or by night, but in all things shall behave himself as a faithful apprentice ought to do. And the said master his said apprentice shall teach and instruct, or cause to be taught and instructed in the art and mystery as mason; finding unto his said apprentice during the said time meat, drink, washing, lodging, and apparel, fitting an apprentice teaching him to read, and allowing him three months towards the latter end of his time to go to school to write, as also double apparel at end of said time. As witness our hands and seals, interchangeably put to two instruments of the same purpose, November the twenty fifth, one thousand six hundred and seventy-six.[18]

It is evident that the phraseology and content were borrowed from the earliest English indentures. The same obligations are laid upon each party to the contract. The apprentice bound himself "to serve and abide" with the master for a certain term, in this case twelve years and five months — presumably until he was twenty-one years of age. Further, he promised to serve "faithfully," keep his master's "lawful secrets," obey his commands, protect him from "damage . . . done of others," and observe proper moral conduct. In return, the master bound himself to provide maintenance, teach the apprentice his trade, and give him double apparel at the end of the term. In addition, in this instance, the master promised to teach the boy to read.

[18] New Hampshire Hist. Soc. Coll. Province Records, 1680–92, Vol. VIII, 287.

This aspect of the master's obligation was not required by law until 1642, and will be considered in a later paragraph.

From the time of the earliest settlements in New England it had been the custom for the master to give his apprentice two suits of clothes at the completion of the period of service. Most of the earlier records of Massachusetts and New Plymouth mention this provision.[19]   In 1641, the "Liberties of the Massachusetts Collonie in New England," required that "Servants that have served diligentlie and faithfully to the benefit of their maisters seaven yeares, *shall not be sent away emptie.*"[20]

If either party to the contract violated his agreement, he was punished by the town authorities.   Masters were permitted to chastise unruly apprentices, but the town usually dealt with such cases in the following manner: "At a Commission Court according to Order Jan'y 18, 1653," Alexander Maxwell, an apprentice, was ordered to be "publicly whipped for abusing his master."[21]   This instance is typical of town action in regard to the punishment of apprentices who broke their covenants.[22]   It was by no means an uncommon thing

[19] Recs. Col. New Plymouth, I, 31.   New Plymouth, 1634: "at the end of the sayd terme the sayd Thomas is to cloth him with two sutes."

Ibid., I, 35.   New Plymouth, 1635: "2 suits."

Ibid., I, 45.   New Plymouth, 1636: "at the expiracon of the said terme, he the said John, to giue him one compleate sute of appel, beside two other one for ordinary weare, & the other for the Sabbath."

Ibid., I, 110.   New Plymouth, 1638: "in thend thereof to giue him double apparell throughout, in convenyent manner, with one suite for Lords dayes, and another for workeing dayes."

Lechford, 151, 162.   Boston, 1639.

[20] Old South Leaflets, Vol. 7, No. 164.

[21] Coll. Maine Hist. Soc., Vol., I, 276.

Records and Files, I, 20.   "Court held at Salem, 29: 7: 1640.   John Cooke, servant to Mr. Wm. Clark of Salem, to be severely whipped and have a shackle put upon his leg for resisting his master's authority."

Ibid., I, 356.   Salem, 27: 4: 1654.

[22] Recs. Col. New Plymouth, I, 15.   "Things done by the Govr & Cowncell betweene July the 1 & October.   July 23, 1635; Will Mendlue, the servt of Will Palmer, whipped for attempting uncleanes with the maid servt of the said Palmer, & for running away from his master being forcibly brought againe by Penwatechet a Manomet Indian."

for an apprentice to "absent himself from his master's service," or in other words, to run away. In this event the master advertised his loss, giving a description of the apprentice, and offering a reward.[23] If apprehended, and brought back, the runaway was obliged to serve a longer time than he had bargained for in the indenture.[24] In some

Ibid., XI, 47. June 4, 1645. "Servant or apprentice . . . that shall steale . . . . his Masters goods shall make double restitucon either by payment or servitude . . . for the first default, and for . . . second default . . . make double restitucon and either fynd sureties for his good bahauior or be whipt."

Ibid., XI, 96. 1655: "It is enacted that . . . servants or children that shall play att Cards or dice for the first offence to bee corrected att the discretion of theire parents or masters and for the 2cond offence to bee publickly whipt."

Records and Files, I, 62. "Court held at Salem, 9:5:1644: John Burridg, a boy apprenticed to Jno Porter . . . to be whipped severely," for stealing from his master.

Ibid., I, 18, 27, 62, 91, 100, 285.

[23] Herald of Freedom, Boston, Tuesday, May 21, 1791. "Run away from the Subscriber in Boston, on the first instant Mathias Fanning an apprentice young man, about nineteen years of age . . . . 6 pence reward. John Magner."

Thomas's Massachusetts Spy or Worcester Gazette, Worcester, Wed., Jan. 4, 1797. "Two Pence Half Penny Reward: Ran away from the subscriber, on the 15th of this month Simon Remington, an indented lad, 16 years of age, about five feet eight inches high, slender built, dark brown hair; had on when he went away a cinnamon coloured coat, Jane waistcoat and overalls, and a round hat. Who ever will take up the said runaway, and return him to his master shall receive the above reward, but no charges paid. All persons are forbid employing or harbouring said runaway, as they wish to avoid the rigour of the law, Petersham, Dec. 26, 1796. Signed Joseph Brown."

Ibid., Wed., Jan. 18, 1797; Wed., Feb. 21, 1798; Wed., Feb. 28, 1798.

[24] Acts and Resolves of Mass. Bay, I, 192. "An Act for Preventing of Men's Sons and Servants Absenting themselves from their Parents or Masters Service without Leave," passed Mar. 14, 1694. Masters of vessels are forbidden to detain any minor or apprentice on penalty of five pounds per week. "Every Apprentice or covenant servant who shall unlawfully absent himself from his master and enter himself on any ship or vessel as aforesaid, with intent to leave his master's service, or continue there more than the space of twenty-four hours, and be thereof convicted before their majesties' justices in general sessions of the peace within the same county, *shall forfeit unto his master such further service*, from and after the expiration of the term which his said master had in him at the time of his departure, as the said court shall order, not exceeding one year."

Ibid., IV, 179. An Act of 1758. "If any apprentice or servant shall elope or desert the service to which he or she is or shall be bound, and damage accrue thereby to the master or mistress of such servants, it shall be lawful for the justices of the court of sessions upon application made to them, to order satisfaction to

cases provision for this was made in the contract.[25]   A fine
was imposed upon persons convicted of "enticing away,"
and "harboring" apprentices.[26]

Masters who maltreated their apprentices or who neglected to provide adequate maintenance, and trade instruction, were fined by the town, and their apprentices
were taken away and bound to other masters.   The early
colonists enacted no legislation on this subject; the English
custom seems to have prevailed.   Later, in 1642, the Selectmen were instructed to inquire into the usage of apprentices,
and "make return" or report to the town meeting.[27]   The
town then determined upon the action to be taken.   Poor-
apprentices were protected by a Massachusetts Bay Act of
1703 which required that "the selectmen or overseers of the
poor shall inquire into the usage of children bound out by
themselves or their predecessors and endeavor to defend them
from any wrongs or injuries."[28]   A general statute of 1758
applying to all apprentices made it "lawful for the courts

be made by such servant or apprentice, either by service or otherwise, as to them
shall seem meet."

Records and Files, I, 286. "Court held at Salem, 30:4:1653. John Robinson servant to Tho. Putnam, to be whipped, and to serve his master one year
longer than his agreement, for frequently running away from his master."

[25] Recs. Col. New Plymouth, I, 129. A Court of Assistants, Aug. 13, 1639:
"if the said Simon do happen to dept his masters service without licence by running
away, the said Simon do pmise to serve the sd Thomas two yeares ouer and aboue
his terme euery tyme hee shall so runn away before the expiracon of the said
terme of seauen yeares."

[26] Records and Files, II, 275. "Court held at Ispwich, Mar. 26, 1661: William
Buckley v. Thamar Quilter. For harboring and withholding his apprentice from
him. Verdict for plaintiff, the boy to be returned."

Ibid., II, 403. "Court held at Salem, June 24, 1662: Thomas Chandler v.
Job Tyler. For taking away his apprentice Hope Tyler, and detaining him out
of his service. Verdict for plaintiff, the boy to be returned."

Acts and Resolves of Mass. Bay, II, 119. Act of Nov. 15, 1716. Masters of
vessels who unlawfully carry away apprentices "shall forfeit the sum of £50."

[27] Records of the Gov. and Col. of Mass. Bay in New England, II, 6.

Records and Files, I, 69. "Court held at Salem, 27:6:1644: Hugh Laskm
and his wife fined 40s for hard usage of his late servant in victuals and clothes
. . . the bed and clothing were not as should be. . . . One time the boy did not
eat until 11 o'clock . Goodman Balch said the boy was growing thin."

[28] Acts and Resolves, Mass. Bay, I, 538.

of general sessions of the peace for the respective counties, upon complaint or representation made by the overseers of the poor or selectmen of any town in such county . . . where any indented, bought or legally bound servant or apprentice have been abused or evil treated by their masters or mistresses" to fine such masters or mistresses five pounds, and take away their apprentices and bind them to other masters.[29]

With the consent of the apprentice the master might sell some years of his service.[30] The apprentice then served the remainder of his term with the new master, who either agreed to observe the terms of the original indenture, or persuaded the boy to enter into a new covenant. Such sales, or assignments, were always registered in the town records. In the event of the master's death before the completion of the term, the apprentice usually served out his term with the heir.[31]

[29] Acts and Resolves, Mass. Bay, IV, 179.

[30] Recs. Col. New Plymouth, I, 132. Sept. 25, 1639: "Mr. Henry Feake of Sandwich, wth and by the consent of Edmund Edwards, his servant hath assigned and made over unto John Barnes, of Plymouth, all the residue of the terme wch by indenture the said Edmond is to serve the sd Mr. Feake to serue it forth wth the said John Barnes, the said John Barnes fynding unto the said Edmond, meate, drinke, lodging & washing, during the terme."

Ibid., I, 158. July 28, 1640: "John Winslow, for and in consideracon of the sum of twelue pounds sterl hath bargained and sould all his interest in the service of Joseph Grosse."

Ibid., I, 15, 16, 65, 102, 107, 129. Dates 1633-40.

Lechford, 151. Boston, 8.6.1639: "Christopher Stanley for £10, 10s Assignes the boy, and all writings concerning him, Richard Bayly, to be bound to Isaake Cullimore of Boston in N. E. Carpenter, his apprentice, to serve him from 24.4. ult. for 7 yeares . . . meate, drinke, & clothes, & Double apparell when he goes forth."

Ibid., 101 (1639), 255 (1640).

Records and Files, I, 187. "Court held at Ispwich, 26:1:1650. Thomas Varnye son of Willm. Varnye, being bound unto Willm. Bartholomew of Ipswich, for fourteen years is now assigned to Mr. Henry Bartholomew of Salem."

Ibid., I, 250. Ipswich, Mar. 30, 1652; II, 132. Salem, Nov. 9, 1658.

Boston News Letter, April 15, 1714; *Ibid.*, April 25, 1715; Boston Evening Post, March 9, 1747, advertise the sale of apprentices' terms.

[31] Records and Files, I, 254. Will dated 30:1:1652: "I giue unto my son in lawe all my right and interest in Thomas Varney my apprentice."

York Records, Book III, Folio 42. An agreement, dated Dec. 9, 1678, between Nicholas Hodgsden and his son mentions an apprentice who is to serve out his term with the son if the father dies.

Indentures were bequeathed as a matter of course, with other property.

The apprenticing of poor-children in the earliest days of the Massachusetts Bay Colony was regulated by the Poor Law of 1601. The children of poor parents were taken away by the town, and placed with masters who would provide adequate maintenance. A Salem town order of 1648 indicates the method of procedure: "It is ordered that the eldest children of Reuben Guppy be placed out, the boy till the age of 21 years and the mayd till the age of 18 years." [32] In such cases the Selectmen became parties to the contract, and the form of indenture was changed to include their names. Such an indenture, of the following century, shows this modification:

This indenture made the fourteenth day of September Anno Domo 1747 by and between Luke Lincoln, Benj. Tuckor, Nathall Goodspeed, & John Whittemor all of Leicester in the county of Worcester selectmen of sd Leicester on the one part, Matthew Scott of Leicester aforesaid yeoman on the other part Witnesseth that the above sd selectmen by virtue of the Law of this province them Impowering & with the assent of two of his Majesties Justices of the Peace for sd county hereto annexed do put and bind out to the sd Matthew Scott & to his Heirs Executors & Adminrs as an Apprentice Moses Love a Minor aged two years and Eight months with him & them to live & dwell with as an apprentice dureing the term of Eighteen years & four months (Viz) untill he shall arrive to the age of twenty-one years . . . he being a poor child & his parents not being able to support it . . . sd apprentice . . . shall . . . serve at such Lawful employment . . . as he shall from time to time . . . be capable of doing . . . & not absent himself from his or their service without Leave & in allthings behaue himself as a good & faithfull apprentice ought to do.[33]

It will be noted that the form observes the English requirement of securing the consent of two justices of the peace.

So far we have considered the general practice of apprenticeship as it existed in New Plymouth and Massachusetts Bay prior to the legislation which changed it from

[32] Felt, Annals of Salem, II, 397.
[33] New England Hist. and Geneal. Register, Vol. 34, 311.

an English practice to one peculiarly American.   As we have noted, from our examination of the records, the essential characteristics of the apprenticeship system were reproduced from the custom of the mother-country.   But with the appearance of new colonial legislation important additions were made.   The scope of apprenticeship was broadened to such an extent that it became a new institution.

CHAPTER III

THE EDUCATIONAL ASPECTS OF THE PRACTICE OF APPRENTICESHIP IN THE NEW PLYMOUTH AND MASSACHUSETTS BAY COLONIES

PERHAPS the earliest legislation concerning apprenticeship in the New England colonies is to be found in an Act of the General Court of the Colony of New Plymouth, dated Sept. 7, 1641. In this Act, "It is enacted That those that have releefe from the townes and have children, and doe not ymploy them, That then it shall be lawfull for the Towneship to take order that those children shall be put to worke in fitting ymployment according to their strength and abilities or placed out by the Townes."[1] It clearly recognised the principle established by the English Poor Law of 1601, that the care of poor-children was a public responsibility. The town met this responsibility by delegating the Selectmen to "place out," or apprentice the children of poor parents "into families where they may be better brought up and provided for."[2] This care included not only the maintenance but also the education of the apprentices. In fact all children whose education had been neglected were provided for by poor and apprenticeship legislation.

---

[1] The Compact with the Charter and Laws of the Colony of New Plymouth, 70. This law was reenacted in 1658 (Recs. Col. New Plymouth, XI, 120).

Records of the Town of New Plymouth, I, 12. "At a Townes meeting holden at Plymouth the Xiiiith of January, 1642. Concerning the placeing and disposing of ffrancis Billingtons children according to the Act and order of the Court, It is ordered and agreed upon that John Cooke . . . shall have Joseph until hee shalbe of the age of twenty one years . . . that his eldest Boy shalbe with John Winslaw . . . until . . . age of XXI years . . . that Gyles Rickett shall take . . . a girle . . . untill she shall accomplish the age of twenty years or be married. . . . That Gabriell ffallowell shall have another . . . a girle . . . untill . . . age of twenty yeares or be marryed."

[2] Compact, 274. Law passed June, 1671.

The emphasis upon education appears very clearly in a New Plymouth Order dated June, 1671:

It is ordered that the Deputies and Selectmen of every Town shall have a vigilant eye from time to time over their Brethren and Neighbours, to see that all Parents and Masters do duely Endeavor, to teach their children and servants as they grow capable, so much learning as through the blessing of God they may attain, *at least to be able to read the Scriptures, and other profitable Books printed in the English Tongue .and the knowledge of the capital Laws* etc. . . . And further that all Parents and Masters do breed and bring up their children and apprentices in some honest lawful calling, labour or employment. . . . That a fine of 10 shillings shall be levied on the goods of negligent Parents and Masters.

And if three months after that, there be no due care taken and continued, for the Education of such children and apprentices as aforesaid, then a fine of 20 shillings shall be levied on such Delinquent's Goods to the Town's use.

And lastly, if in three months after that, there be no due Reformation of the said neglect, then the said Selectmen with the help of two Magistrates, shall take such children and servants from them and place them with some Masters for years (boyes till they come to twenty-one, and girls eightteen years of age) which will more strictly educate and govern them according to the rules of this Order.[3]

At an earlier date, the Massachusetts Bay Colony passed a similar but more comprehensive law, which applied to all districts or plantations in the colony:

At a General Court of Elections held at Boston, on June 14, 1642.

This court taking into consideration the great neglect in many parents and masters in training up their children in labor and learning and other employments which may be profitable to the Commonwealth, do hereupon order and decree that in every town the chosen men appointed for managing the prudential affairs of the same shall henceforth stand charged with the care and redress of this evil, so they shall be liable to be punished and fined for the neglect thereof upon any presentment of the grand jurors or other information or complaint in any plantation in this jurisdiction; and for this end they or the greater part of them, shall have power to take account from time to time of their parents and masters of their children concerning their calling and employment of their children, especially their ability to read and understand the principles of religion and the capital laws of the country, and to impose

---

[3] Compact, 271.

fines upon all those who refuse to render such accounts to them when required; and they shall have power, with the consent of any court or any magistrate *to put forth apprentices the children of such as shall not be able and fit to employ and bring them up, nor shall take care to dispose of them themselves;* and they are to take care that such as are set to keep cattle be set to some other employment withal as spinning upon the rock, knitting, weaving tape, etc; and that boys and girls be not allowed to converse together so as to occasion any wanton, dishonest or immodest behavior.   And for their better performance of this trust committed to them they may divide the town amongst them, appointing to every of the said townmen a certain number of families to have oversight of.[4]

Our Puritan forefathers were familiar with the English practice as established by the laws of 1562 and 1601, and recognised its·shortcomings. The Statute of Artificers provided for the industrial training of youth, but did not take into consideration the need of even the rudiments of education for the lower classes. The Poor Law of 1601 made no pretense of providing anything but a home for those bound out, and as a natural consequence thousands of Poor Law apprentices were exploited in "blind-alley" occupations. To protect their new commonwealth from the evils arising from such imperfect legislation, the Massachusetts Bay colonists insisted (1) that masters must teach, or "cause to be taught," their apprentices to read; and (2) that apprentices must be trained in "employments which may be profitable to the Commonwealth."[5] No useless occupations, such as minding cattle, were to be tolerated; apprenticeship was not a scheme of exploitation, but was essentially an educational institution.

Before 1642 the English law obtained in the matter of regulating apprenticeship, but now apprenticeship was seen to possess new and broader possibilities of use. Not only was it viewed as a mode of poor-relief, and of keeping up the supply of skilled labor, but it was also considered a means of compelling the education of all youth. To include this

[4] Recs. of the Gov. and Col. of Mass. Bay in New England, II, 6.

[5] Mass. Bay Act of 1642. Compare the New Plymouth Order of 1671: "that all Parents and Masters do breed and bring up their children and apprentices in some honest lawful calling, labour or employment."

Acts and Resolves of the Prov. of Mass. Bay, I, 67. Mass. Bay Act of 1692.

added feature new legislation was necessary, the type of which is represented by the Massachusetts Bay Order of 1642, and the New Plymouth measure of 1671. In these Orders the obligation was laid upon all parents, rich and poor, as well as masters, to teach their children to read. The Selectmen were required to visit the homes of parents and masters, and ascertain if the children had been taught or were being taught.[6] Those who failed to comply with the

[6] In 1642 Cambridge divided its territory among the Selectmen so that one would be responsible for each portion in carrying out the Order of the General Court (Cambridge Records, 47). In 1670 the Selectmen issued an order dividing the town into eight districts, and assigning two persons to each district "for the Cattichising the youth of the towne." (*Ibid.*, 188)

Hazen, History of Billerica, 252. Billerica, 1661: "the townsmen do agree that Lieut. Will French and Ralph Hill, senior, do take care and examine the several families in our town whether their children and servants are taught in the precepts of religion in reading and learning their catechism."

Ibid., 252. The Selectmen "appoint the next second day to go the rounds to examine the teaching of children and youth according to the law."

Watertown Records, I, 204. "Jenvry the 3d 1670. At a meeting of the select men at the house of Isaake Sterns: It was further agreed that the select men should goe thrugh the town in their ceueral quarters to make tryall whether children and servants be educated in Learneing to read the English tongue and in the Knowledg of the capitall Laws according to the Law of the Country also that they may be educated in sum orthadox Catacise."

Ibid., I, 114. Nov. 25, 1672: "Nathan fisk John whitney and Isaak mickstur meaking return of thear inquiry aftur childrens edducation finde that John fisks chilldren ear naythur taught to read nor yet thear caticise."

The Royal Colony of New Hampshire, whose early legislation borrowed much from the Mass. Bay laws, imposed a similar duty upon its Selectmen in an Act passed May 10, 1710: "fforasmuch as Ignorance, ill Manners and Irreligion are propagated by many parents and Masters by Neglecting to Instruct Youth under their Care et: It shall be Lawfull for the Selectmen with a Justice of the Peace to examine all Youth of Tenn Years of Age whether they shall have been taught to Read and All those which cannot Read at Said Age to binde out to good Masters who shall be Obleidged to Learn them to Read and write till they shall be of Age." (Laws of New Hampshire, II, 115)

Sometimes the Selectmen delegated the duty of visiting and catechising to the ministers. Billerica, in 1675, records: "In reference to the catechising of the youth of the town and examining them concerning their reading, a duty imposed on the Selectmen by the Honorable Court, to take care that children and youth be instructed in both: the selectmen do order that all children and youth, single persons from eight years old and upward, their parents and masters shall send such children and servants to the Rev. Mr. Samuel Whiting, at such times as shall afterwards be appointed by him, to be examined of both, as hoping this might be

law were first warned, and in case of continued neglect they were punished by a fine, or their children were taken away from them by the Selectmen, and bound out to "Masters for years (boyes till they come to twenty-one and girls eightteen years of age) which will more strictly educate and govern them."[7]   In cases of neglect on the part of the well-

a good expedient for the encouragement of all superiors and youth." (Hazen, History of Billerica, 272) In 1680 the Selectmen of Dorchester appointed "Elder Humphrey to Cattechiz the youth and Children." (Boston Records, IV, 255)

[7] New Plymouth Act of 1671.

A complaint of neglect and subsequent promise of reparation appear in Watertown, in 1671: "At a meeting of the selectmen at Willyam Bond his house sept. 2n: 1671.   Ther comeing a complaint of a child of Willyam Knop that haue ben neglected in being Learned in the English tongue we did apoint John Bigulah to warn in Thomas Smyth to the meeting of the selectmen also to warn willyam knop to the meeting." (Watertown Records, I, 107)

Ibid., 109.   "At a meeting of the selectmen at Thomas Fleg seni his house october 24th 1671: Thomas Smyth a peereing before the selectmen a bought the Daughter of Willyam knop did acknowlidg that the child had not ben so well a tended in matter of Learneing as she should haue ben: did promise that he would be mor carfull for the time to come that she shall be Learned in the knowlidg of reading the english tongue."

Boston Records, VII, 67.   25:1:1672, "At a meetinge (held in Boston) . . . It was ordered that notice be given to the seuerall psons vnder-written that they within one moneth after the date hereof dispose of theire seuerall Childrenn (herein nominated or mentioned) to serue by Indentures for some terme of yeares, according to their ages and capacities; wch if they refuse or neglect to doe the Magistrates and Selectmen will take theire said Children from them, and place them with such Masters as they shall prouide accordinge as the lawe directs.   And that they doe accordinge to this ordr dispose of their Children doe make returne of the names of Mastrs & Children soe put out to seruice, with theire Indentures to the Selectmen at theire nexte monethly Meeting beinge the last Monday in Aprill next."   List of names follows.

Lancaster Records, 96.   Lancaster, April 7, 1674: "The Court do commend it to the care of the selectmen of yt place dilligent to inspect his family and observe their manner for the future, and in case they find not an amendment in their charges whereof he hath been now convicted they are hereby ordered and impowered to dispose of his sonne to service where he may be better taught & governed."

Watertown Records, I, 102.   "At a generall towne meeteing Nov. 7, 1670. Ordered that John Edy seir shall goe to John Fisk his house and to George Lorance and Willyam preist houseis to inquir a bought their Children wither they be Lerned to read the english tong and in case they be defective to warne in the said John George and Willyam to the next meeting of the selectmen."

Ibid., I, 103.   Dec. 13, 1670, "Willyam preist John Fisk and George Lorance

to-do, or those who were capable of giving instruction, the law required that they be placed out "as when parents are indigent and rated as nothing to the public taxes." [8] Selectmen, or "prudential men," who were delinquent in this duty "shall be liable to be punished and fined . . . upon any presentment of the grand jurors or other information or complaint in any plantation in this jurisdiction." [9]

Naturally not all masters were capable of teaching their apprentices to read. The records give abundant evidence of the illiteracy of masters in general. Most of them were obliged to make marks in lieu of signatures to legal documents, and most of them must have resorted to the Town Clerk or to a schoolmaster in order to have the simplest kind of communication composed and written.[10] But, according to the law, all children must be given this elementary education. Illiterate masters were obliged, therefore, to send their apprentices to persons who could teach them, which, in most cases, meant that they sent the apprentices to schools. Several elementary schools had already appeared

being warned to a meeting of the select men at John Bigulah his house they making their a peerance: and being found defecttiue weer admonished for not Learning their Children to read the english toung: weer convinced did acknowledg their neglect and did promise a mendment."

[8] Acts and Resolves of the Prov. of Mass. Bay, II, 756. "An Act for employment and providing for the Poor of the Town of Boston," passed July 3, 1735.

[9] Mass. Bay Act of 1642.

A presentment occurs in a Commission Court, held July 6, 1675, in Maine; "We present the Selectmen of the Town for not taking care that the children and youth of the Town be taught their Catechism and educated according to the Law." (Maine Hist. Soc. Coll., I, 285)

"We present the Selectmen of the town of Kittery for not taking care that their children and youth be taught their catechism and educated according to the Law." "We present the Selectmen of Cape Porpus for not taking care that their children and youth of the town be taught their catechism and educated according to the law." "We present the Selectmen of Scarborough for not taking care that the children and youth of the town be taught and educated according to the Law." "We present the Selectmen of the town of Falmouth for not taking care that the children and youth of the town of Falmouth be taught their catechism and educated according to the law." (See Appendix B)

[10] Even if they secured the services of the Town Clerk they could not be sure of receiving a perfect piece of workmanship; the chirography of most of these worthies was barely legible, and the spelling was equally wretched.

in the New Plymouth and Massachusetts Bay Colonies, and later, in 1647, the Massachusetts General Court "ordered that every township in this jurisdiction, after the Lord has increased them to the number of fifty householders, shall forthwith appoint one within their number to teach all such children as shall resort to him to write and read, whose wages shall be paid either by the parents or masters of such children, or by the inhabitants in general, by way of supply, as the major part of those that order the prudentials of the town shall appoint."[11]

To enforce a law compelling universal education, the town was forced to assume the responsibility of providing the means. In order to relieve the town of expense, the Selectmen, in binding out poor-children or the children of those who neglected to provide the instruction required by law, endeavored to find masters who not only could furnish "meat, drink and lodging," but, in addition, could teach or afford to pay for tuition.[12] Failing in the latter the Selectmen made a bargain or agreement with the prospective master to take an apprentice for a certain sum of money to be paid out of the town rate.[13] This money was to be expended in main-

[11] Mass. Col. Recs., II, 203.

Plymouth Colony Records, XI, 246. Plymouth, in a law passed 1677, made a similar provision.

Acts and Resolves of the Prov. of Mass. Bay, I, 63. In 1693 Mass. Bay repeated the law of 1647.

[12] Dedham Records, IV, 203. Dated 20:11:1670. The Selectmen were instructed to see "if it (the child) could be put out without charge."

[13] Dorchester Records, 306. Dated 1651. "It is agreed between the Selectmen and be Tolman that hee shall take Henry lakes child to keepe it untill it com to 21 yeares of age &c and therefore to haue 26 pounds and to give security to the town and to teach it to read and wright and when it is capable if he lives the said br Tolman to teach it his trade."

Watertown Records, I, 56.

Dorchester Records, 165. Dated 1669. "the foresaid Selectmen doe in behalf of themselves for the time being and their successors on the behalf of the Town that ther shall be paid out of the towne Rate the Sum of Thirty pound Viz: ten pounds at the end of the feirst yecr after the date hereof whether the Child liue or dy; and ten pound by the yeer for the next two yeers then the said Merefield shall haue but p'portionable of the pay according to the life of the Child."

Watertown Records, I, 104. Jan. 17, 1670, Thomas Fleg and John Bigulah

taining and educating the apprentice. If the apprentice died before completing his period of service, the master must remit part of the money according to a schedule agreed upon with the Selectmen: Dorchester, 1651, "further agreed if it (the apprentice) dies within 2 months br Tolman (the master) is to returne 21 pounds if it die at one yeares end br. T. is to returne 18 pounds, etc." [14]

Another mode of providing education for all was that of abating "wholly or in part" for the poor the charges of instruction. Where free schools had not yet appeared, all pupils must pay for tuition, and contribute toward the rate for the support of the town school. The poor, however, were taken care of by the town; the Selectmen, and later the Overseers of the Poor, were instructed to ascertain how much of the school rates and tuition charges certain people could afford to pay. Some were exempted entirely, and others were obliged to pay according to their means, — "the selectmen Being Judges of that matter." [15]

---

were instructed by the town "a bought puting out of a child to be an a prentice with Mr. Nuenson, and to drive a bargen a bought it if they can." *Ibid.*, I, 107. Sept. 2, 1671: Thomas Fleg and John Bigulah "put out the oldist of the two of a matter of eight yeers of age to John Fleg as a prentice till she be of eighteen yeers of age the said John Fleg was to haue heer well pareled at her comeing to him and to haue for his incurigment fifty shillings to be paid by the town."

Corey, History of Malden, 402. 1745, "Voated that Edward Wayte shall have John Ramsdell who is about five years old till he come of age and said Wayt shall have thirty pounds old tenor with him in case said Waitt wil be obliged to learne the child to read, wright, and cypher and also to learne him the Shoemakers trade."

[14] Dorchester Records, 306. 1651.

[15] 1686, Watertown. "Voated Allso that the Towne will paye for such Children as thear parents are not abell to pay for the select men Being Judges of that matter." (Watertown Records, II, 28)

1687, Brookline. "Voted that for the Annual maintainance of the Schoolmaster twelve pounds per annum in or as money be Raised equally by a Rate accordinge to the usual manner of Raising publick charges by the three men And that the Remainder necessary to support the charge of the Master be laid equally on the scholars heads *save any persons that are poor to be abated wholly or in part.*" (Muddy River and Brookline Records, 86)

1702, Braintree. "Provided that any poor person in this Town who shall send any children to sd school & find themselves unable to pay upon application

In addition to these means of making universal elementary education possible, many towns established free schools.[16] These schools offered to all children without cost the rudiment required by law. Some, in answer to the growing demand for a more complete education, taught reading, writing, and cyphering. Town action on this matter was supplemented in many instances by bequests from charitable individuals for the purpose of establishing free schools.

An elementary education limited to reading, the "principles of religion," and "the capital laws of the country," could not long satisfy the needs of a growing colony. Soon there appeared a demand for the addition of writing and cyphering, or "casting accounts." We find many records which show how the need of these practical subjects was met:

to the Select men it shall be in their power to remit a part or ye whole of ye sum." (Braintree Records, 51)

1703, Boston. "Ordered that a vote be prepared to empower Overseers to advance of ye Town Stock towards teaching the Children to read of such parents who are extreamly poor." (Boston Records, XI, 33)

1705, Plymouth. "The Children of such as through poverty are rendered oncapable to pay theire Children to goe to school free." (Recs. of the Town of Plymouth, II, 2)

1707, Springfield. "agreed that sd Selectmen do exempt their Parents & Masters (of poor children) from paying for such children going to school   In whole or in part." (First Century of the History of Springfield, II, 74)

[16] Watertown, 1670. (Watertown Records, I, 102)

Boston, 1679. "Afree school to teach the children of poore people." (Boston Records, VII, 127)

Boston, 1682. "The same day it was voted by ye inhabitants yt the same Comittee with ye Select men consider of & pvide one or more Free Schooles for the teachinge Children to write and Cypher within this towne." (Boston Records, VII, 157)

Boston, 1690. "Ordered that Mr. John Cole be allowed to keep a free school for reading and writing and that ye selectmen agree with him for his salary." (Boston Records, VII, 200)

Brookline, 1700. "It was voted that the Selectmen should provide a Schoolmaster for them, To teach their children to read, write & cypher & order his pay out of the Town Treasury." (Muddy River and Brookline Records, 63)

Malden, 1701. "The school is to be free for all ye inhabitants of ye town." (Corey, History of Malden, 602)

Duxbury, 1741. "The school shall be a free school for the whole town." (Duxbury Records, 270)

in 1651, a master of Dorchester agrees with the Selectmen to teach his apprentice "to read and wright"; [17] on April 2, 1667, Boston gives "Mr. Will Howard liberty to keep a wrighting schoole, to teach childeren to writte and keep accounts"; [18] a York, Maine, indenture, dated Sept. 16, 1674, witnesses the covenant of a master to teach his apprentice "to write & siffer"; [19] in a Portsmouth, New Hampshire, indenture, dated Nov. 25, 1676, the master promises to teach his apprentice to "read, and allowing him three months toward the latter end of his time to go to school to write"; [20] on Mar. 27, 1677, one Joseph Underwood of Watertown promises the Selectmen to teach his apprentice "to read and wright and sum authortox cattacise." [21] Parents and Selectmen, in binding out children, were everywhere demanding that masters provide instruction in reading, writing, and cyphering, and these subjects soon came to constitute the customary elementary curriculum.

The evidence exhibited in the preceding paragraph presents the answers to a felt demand for a more comprehensive training than colony or town action had yet stipulated. But, although there existed a fairly widespread recognition of this need, not all children shared equally in the distribution of this more complete tuition. Many masters still gave

[17] Dorchester Records, 165.

[18] Boston Records, VII, 36.

Recs. of the Town of Plymouth, I, 270. "At a Town Meeting held at plimouth July 31, 1699 voted that the selectmen should take care to provide A scoole Master . . . & that Every Schollar that Coms to *wrigh or syfer* or to learn latten shall pay 3 pence pr weke if to Read only then to pay 3 half pence per weke to be paid by their Masters or parents."

[19] York Deeds, Book II, Folio 159.

Ibid., Bk. II, Folio 129. Indenture dated April 4, 1672. Master covenants to teach his apprentice "to reade & writte."

Ibid., Bk. III, Folio 12. Indenture dated Oct. 5, 1676. Master to teach his apprentice "to read and write."

Ibid., Bk. III, Folio 73. Indenture dated March 4, 1679. Master to teach his apprentice "to write &c: read, Legably & audibly."

[20] New Hampshire Hist. Soc. Coll. Province Records, 1680–1692, Vol. VIII, 287.

[21] Watertown Records, I, 129.

their apprentices only the instruction demanded by the law of 1642. New legislation was needed, therefore, to establish uniformity of procedure in the matter, to compel all masters to furnish the three R's. Such action was forthcoming, however, and legislation enacted between the years 1703 and 1771 indicates the development of the educational requirement.

On Nov. 16, 1692 the town of Boston passed "An Act for regulating Townships, choice of Town Officers and setting forth their power" which ordered the "overseers of the poor or selectmen where there are no other persons especially chosen and appointed to be overseers of the poor . . . with the assent of two justices of the peace, to bind any poor children belonging to such town to be apprentices where they shall see convenient, a man-child until he shall come to the age of twenty-one years, and a woman-child to the age of eighteen years, or time of marriage; which shall be as effective to all intents and purposes as if any such child were of full age and by indenture or covenant had bound him or herself." [22] The education of these apprentices in reading at least was assured by the Act of 1642, but this, as we have seen, had been outgrown. Recognition of the need of writing was made in a Poor Law of Nov. 27, 1703, which reads:

An Act of Supplement to the Acts Referring to the Poor.

Whereas the law for the binding out of poor children apprentices is misconstrued by some to extend only to such children whose parents receive alms; for explanation thereof,

Be it declared and enacted by his Excellency the Governor, Council and Representatives in General Court assembled, and by the authority of the same,

That the selectmen or overseers of the poor in any town or district within this province, or the greater part of them, shall take order and are hereby impowered from time to time, by and with the assent of two justices of the peace, to set to work, or bind out apprentices as they shall think convenient, all such children whose parents shall by the selectmen or overseers of the poor, or the greater part of them, be thought unable to maintain them (whither they receive alms, or are chargeable

[22] Acts and Resolves of the Prov. of Mass. Bay, I, 67.

to the place or not), so as they be not sessed to publick taxes or assessments for the province or town charges; male children till they come to the age of twenty-one years, and females till they come to the age of eighteen years, or time of marriage; which shall be as good and effectual in law to all intents and purposes as if any such child were of full age, and by indenture of covenant had bound him or herself, or that their parents were consenting thereto: *provision therein to be made for the instructing of children so bound out, to read and write*, if they be capable. And the selectmen or overseers of the poor shall inquire into the usage of children bound out by themselves or their predecessors and endeavor to defend them from any wrongs or injuries.[23]

The text of this Act clearly makes the same provision — "to read and write" — for both girl- and boy-apprentices, but it is evident that this was not intended, for "An Act for Explanation of and Supplement to the Act referring to the Poor," passed June 19, 1710, amended the stipulation to read: "males to read and write, females to read." [24] The Act of 1710 was repeated Nov. 16, 1720,[25] April 2, 1731,[26] April 10, 1741,[27] and Aug. 8, 1741; the last supplementary Act, however, added to the earlier requirements "males to read, write and cypher, females to read." [28] Finally, on July 4, 1771, "An Act in Addition to the several Acts or Laws of this Province Impowering the Selectmen or Overseers of the Poor of Towns to bind poor children Apprentices," stated the general requirement in its most comprehensive form: "males, reading, writing, cyphering; females, reading, writing." [29]

[23] Acts and Resolves of theProv. of Mass. Bay, I, 538.

[24] *Ibid.*, I, 654.

[25] *Ibid.*, II, 182.

[26] *Ibid.*, II, 597.

[27] *Ibid.*, II, 1053.

New England Hist. and Geneal. Register, Vol. 34, 311. Leiscester, Mass. indenture dated 1747 contains the master's covenant to teach apprentice "to read & write & siffer."

[28] Acts and Resolves of the Prov. of Mass. Bay, II, 1067.

[29] *Ibid.*, V, 161.

Laws of Vermont (Windsor, 1825), 377. Act passed Mar. 3, 1797. Overseers of the poor are to apprentice "poor children, males till they arrive at the age

The educational provisions of the Act of 1642 were re-enforced and amplified by the Poor Laws just reviewed. While these laws were primarily intended to take care of poor children, they applied to all children just as the earlier law did. Children whose education had been neglected were treated as poor-children and bound out accordingly. This is stated very explicitly in a Poor Law enacted July 3, 1735:

An Act for employing and providing for the Poor of the Town of Boston.

And forasmuch as there is great negligence in sundry persons as to the instructing and educating their children, to the great scandal of the Christian name, and of dangerous consequence to the rising generation ... be it enacted.

That where persons bring up their children in such gross ignorance that they do not know, or are not able to distinguish the alphabet of twenty-four letters, at the age of six years, in such case the overseers of the poor are hereby impowered and directed to put or bind out in good families such children, for a decent and Christian education, *as when parents are indigent and rated nothing to the publick taxes,* unless the children are judged incapable, through some inevitable infirmity.[30]

In 1758 Massachusetts Bay enacted a Poor Law which protected from abuse and neglect in the matter of education all apprentices who did not reside "within any town or district." Outlying districts came within the jurisdiction of the general colony legislation.

It shall and may be lawful for the Courts of general sessions of the peace for the respective counties, upon complaint or representation made by the overseers of the poor or selectmen of any town in such county, or by the overseers appointed for the county, where any indented, bought, or ... legally bound, servant or apprentice shall not be within any town or district, that any such servants or apprentices have been abused or

of 21 years, and females till they arrive at the age of 18 years ... *males to be instructed to read, and write, and females to read.*"

Revised Statutes of Vermont, 1839, p. 345. "Overseers of the Poor may bind as apprentices or servants, the minor children of any poor person ... females until the age of 18 years, and males untill the age of 21 years; and provision to be made in the contract for teaching such children to read, write and cypher."

[30] Acts and Resolves of the Prov. of Mass. Bay II, 756. Boston divided into 12 wards, and an Overseer of the Poor appointed for each ward.

evil treated by their masters or mistresses, or that *the education of such children in reading or writing and cyphering, according to the tenor of their indentures, has been unreasonably neglected,* to take cognizance of such representation or complaint, and if upon inquiry there shall appear to have been just cause therefor such master or mistress shall forfeit a sum not exceeding five pounds, for the use of the poor of the town or district where such master or mistress shall then be inhabitant . . . and *the said court may order such child or children to be liberated or discharged from their masters or mistresses, and any male so discharged being under the age of twenty-one years, and any female under the age of eighteen years, may, by order of such court, be bound to other persons until they arrive to the age of twenty-one or eighteen years, respectively.*[31]

The Massachusetts General Court Order of 1642 insisted not only upon parents and masters "training up their children in learning," but also in "labor." Idleness was strictly prohibited,[32] and parents and masters, in employing children, must select only those "employments which may be profitable to the Commonwealth." The Selectmen were directed to "take account from time to time of their parents and masters and of their children, concerning their calling and employment . . . *and they are to take care that such (children) as are set to keep cattle be set to some other employment,*" *in addition,* "as spinning up on the rock, knitting, weaving tape, etc." In the preceding year, Sept. 7, 1641, a General Court held in the New Plymouth colony enacted that the children of "those that have releefe from the townes . . . shall be put to work in *fitting imploy-ment* according to their strength and abilities or placed out by the Townes."[33] This order was repeated in 1658,[34] and in 1671 the New Plymouth General Court demanded that all "Parents and Masters do breed and bring up their children and apprentices in *some honest lawful calling, labour or em-*

---

[31] Acts and Resolves of the Prov. of Mass. Bay, IV, 179.

[32] Recs. of the Col. of New Plymouth, I, 106. "Att a Generall Court held at New Plymouth the fourth Day of December 1638: John Wakefield psented for liueing out of service hath tyme giuen him to puide him a master."

[33] Compact, New Plymouth, 70.

[34] Recs. of the Col. of New Plymouth, 120.

ployment." [35]   A more complete statement of this principle occurs in a Boston law of 1692, in which the Overseers of the Poor, or Selectmen were directed "to take care that *all children*, youth, and other persons of able body living within the town, or precincts thereof (not having estates otherwise to maintain themselves) do not live idly or mispend their time in loitering but that they *be brought up or employed in some honest calling, which may be profitable to themselves and to the publick.*" [36]

Evidently the colonists were determined not to repeat the experience of the mother-country with the problem of vagabondage. The statute books of most of the colonies are copiously punctuated with laws for the suppression of "vagabonds, idle and disorderly persons."

Space will not permit the inclusion of the complete record of the practice of this legislation.   A few examples read as follows:

Salem, Mass., 1644: "Thomas Gooldsmith is to take a son of George Harris about 8 years old, as an apprentice for 12 years to teach him his trade." [37]

Watertown, Mass., Jan. 3, 1656: John Baal agrees with the Selectmen to teach his apprentice the trade of "weauing." [38]

Watertown, Mass., Mar. 3, 1670: "We (the Selectmen) haue therefore a greed to put out two of his children in sum honist famelleys wher they may be educated and brought up in the knowledge of God and sum honist calling." [39]

Leicester, Mass., Sept. 14, 1747: The Selectmen bind out a two year old boy who "shall serve at such Lawfull employment as he shall from time to time be capable of doing." [40]

Danvers, Mass., Feb. 14, 1757: Overseers of the Poor bind out a boy to Elisha Flint who promises to teach "ye said Ezra or cause him to be taught the Art, Trade or Mystery of a Wheelwright." [41]

Another important aspect of the law of 1642 was its emphasis upon good conduct; the Selectmen were instructed to

[35] Compact, New Plymouth, 271.
[36] Acts and Resolves of the Prov. of Mass. Bay, I, 67.
[37] Felt, Annals of Salem, II, 396.
[38] Watertown Records, I, 50.
[39] *Ibid.*, I, 105.
[40] New England Hist. and Geneal. Register, Vol. 34, 311.
[41] Hist. Coll. Essex Institute, II, 90.

see "that boys and girls be not suffered to converse together, so as may occasion any wanton, dishonest or immodest behavior." This was not alone an expression of Puritanism, it was also a reproduction of the English attitude in regard to the behavior of apprentices. English gild and municipal legislation of an early date insist upon proper conduct on the part of apprentices, and masters were held responsible. Early indentures of apprenticeship, which, to some extent, reveal the practice, are very explicit in their proscription of immorality.[42] This emphasis was not repeated in the laws of 1562 and 1601, although they borrowed much from the earlier practice of apprenticeship. In spite of the omission, however, the prohibitions persisted in the practice of the mother-country.[43] The Massachusetts Bay indentures, in their reference to conduct, reproduce verbatim the phraseology of their English models.[44]

[42] Archaeological Journal, XXIX, 184. English indenture of apprenticeship dated 1396. "Tabernam, scortum, talos, aleas, et joca similia non frequentabit. . . . Fornicationem nec adulterium . . . nullo modo committet."

Hibbert, Inf. and Devel. of Eng. Gilds, 52. English indenture dated 1414. "Tabernam, scortum, talos, aleas, et joca similia non frequentabit. . . . Fornicationem nec adulterium cum aliqua muliere de domo et familia dicti Johannis nullo modo committet."

Rogers, Hist. Agric. and Prices, IV, 98. English indenture dated 1451. "He is not to frequent taverns, nor to commit fornication in or out of his master's house. He is not to play at dice, tables, or chequers, or any other unlawful games, but is to conduct himself soberly, justly, piously, well and honorably."

[43] Dunlop, English Apprenticeship, 352. English indenture dated Jan. 6, 1708. "Tavernes or Alehouses hee shall not haunt Dice Cardes or any other unlawfull games hee shall not use ffornication with any woman hee shall not committ."

[44] New Hampshire Hist. Soc. Coll., VIII, 287. A New Hampshire (New Hampshire was part of Mass. Bay 1641–1679) indenture dated Nov. 25, 1676. "Fornication he shall not commit. . . . He shall not play cards, or dice, or any other unlawful game . . . taverns he shall not haunt."

New England Hist. and Geneal. Register, Vol. 33, 18. A Scituate indenture dated Sept. 9, 1751. "Taverns or Ale-houses she shall not frequent; at cards, Dice or any other unlawful Game she shall not play; Fornication she shall not commit."

Diary of Cotton Mather, 199. On April 12, 1713, Cotton Mather made this entry in his diary: "My kinsmen, that are prentices, must have my frequent Counsils and Charges, to shun evil Doings by which young men undo themselves, and to serve their Masters with all possible fidelity."

CHAPTER IV

APPRENTICESHIP AND APPRENTICESHIP EDUCA-
TION IN THE CONNECTICUT, NEW HAVEN,
AND RHODE ISLAND COLONIES

CONNECTICUT AND NEW HAVEN

THE first legislation concerning elementary education in the Connecticut colony is contained in the Code of 1650. It is evident that this Code borrowed much from the 1642 and 1647 laws of Massachusetts, from which colony Connecticut was an off-shoot.[1] In addition to the provisions for an elementary school in every town of fifty families (Cf. Mass. Bay Act of 1647), the statute of 1650, like the Massachusetts law of 1642, made use of the apprenticeship system to compel all parents and masters to educate their children and apprentices. The Code follows:

Forasmuch as the good education of children is of singular behalf and benefit to any commonwealth, and whereas many parents and masters are too indulgent and negligent of their duty in that kind; it is therefore ordered by this Court and authority thereof, that the selectmen of every town, in the several precincts and quarters where they dwell, shall have a vigilant eye over their brethren and neighbors, to see first, that none of them shall suffer so much barbarism in any of their families as not to endeavor to teach by themselves or others their children and apprentices so much learning as may enable them perfectly to read the English tongue and knowledge of the capital laws, upon penalty of twenty shillings for each neglect therein; also, that all masters of fami-

---

[1] Much of the legislation of Connecticut and New Haven was borrowed from Massachusetts Bay Laws. The tenor of earlier laws in these colonies shows that Massachusetts models were used. In 1655, the General Court of New Haven "further desired the Governor to send for one of the new Books of laws of the Massachusetts colony, and to view over a small book of laws newly come from New England which is said to be Mr. Cotton's, and to add to what is already done as he shall think fit." (Records of the Colony of New Haven, 146)

lies do once a week at least catechise their children and servants in the grounds and principles of religion and if any be unable to do so much, that then, at the least, they procure such children and apprentices to learn some short orthodox catechism, without book, that they may be able to answer the questions that shall be propounded to them out of such catechisms by their parents or masters or any of the selectmen when they shall call them to a trial of what they have learned in this kind. And further, that all parents and masters do breed and bring up their children and apprentices in some honest Lawful labor or employment, either in husbandry, or in some other trade profitable to themselves and the commonwealth, if they will not or can not train them up in learning to fit them for higher employments. And if any of the selectmen, after admonition by them given to such masters of families, shall find them still negligent of their duties in the particulars aforementioned, whereby children and servants become rude, stubborn, and unruly, *the said select-men with the help of two magistrates shall take such children or apprentices from them and place them with some masters for years, boys till they come to twenty-one and girls to eighteen years of age complete which will more strictly look unto, and force them to submit unto government, according to the rules of this order,* if by fair means and former instructions they will not be drawn unto it.[2]

After the manner of the 1642 law, this statute required that all children be taught to read, understand the principles of religion and capital laws, and trained in some useful calling. The Connecticut law added the requirement that "all masters of families do once a week at least catechise their children and servants in the grounds and principles of religion." Furthermore, the Selectmen were instructed to "call" children "to a trial of what they have learned in this kind." Parents and masters who neglected to educate their children and apprentices, were to be fined for first offences, and in case of continued neglect, their children or apprentices

---

[2] Conn. Col. Recs., I, 520–21.

An act of 1796 repeats the order that "All parents and masters of children, shall by themselves or others teach and instruct, or cause to be taught and instructed all such children as are under their care and government, according to their ability, to read the English tongue well and to know the laws against capital offenses; And if unable to do so much, then at best to learn some short catechism without book, so as to be able to answer to the questions that shall be propounded to them out of such catechism, of what they have learned of that kind." (Laws of Conn., 1796, 60)

were to be taken away by the Selectmen and bound out to masters who would observe the law.   The Connecticut law also defined the term of service — "boys till they come to twenty-one and girls to eighteen years" — which was omitted in the law of 1642.   In the Massachusetts statute Selectmen who neglected their duty were punished by fines, but no such provision appears in the 1650 Code.   This was amended, however, by the revision of 1702.

In 1655 the New Haven colony enacted a similar, but more conservative law.

Whereas too many parents and masters, either through an over tender respect to their own occasions, and business, or not duly considering the good of their children and apprentices, have too much neglected duty in their education, while they are young and capable of learning, it is ordered That the deputies for the particular court, in each plantation within this jurisdiction for the time being: or where there are no such deputies, the constable or other officers in publick trust, shall from time to time have a vigilant eye over their brethren and neighbours, within the limits of the said plantation, that all parents and masters, doe duly endeavour, either by their own ability and labour, or by improving such schoolmaster, or other helps and means, as the plantation doth afford, or the family may conveniently provide, that all their children and apprentices as they grow capable, may through God's blessing attain at least so much, as to be able duly to read the Scriptures, and other good and profitable printed books in the English tongue, being their native language, and in some competent measure to understand the main grounds and principles of Christian Religion necessary to salvation.   And to give a due answer to such plain and ordinary questions, as may by the said deputies or officers or others, be propounded concerning the same. And where such deputies or officers, whether by information or examination, shall find any parent or master, one or more negligent, he or they shall first give warning, and if thereupon due reformation follow, if the said parents or masters shall thenceforth seriously and constantly apply themselves to their duty in manner before expressed, the former neglect may be passed by; but if not, then the said deputies or other officer or officers, shall three months after such warning, present each such negligent person, or persons, to the next plantation court, where every such delinquent upon proof, shall be fined ten shillings to the plantation, to be levied as other fines.   And if in any plantation, there be kept no such court for the present, in such case, the constable or other officer, or officers, warning such person or persons, before the freemen, or so many of them as upon notice shall meet together, and proving the neglect after warn-ing, shall have power to levy the fine aforesaid. The delinquent (with-out any further private warning) shall be proceeded against as before, but the fine doubled. And lastly, if after the said warning, and fine paid and levied, the said deputies, officer or officers shall find a continuance of the former negligence, if it be not obstinacy, so that such children or servants may be in danger to grow barbarous, rude, and stubborn, through ignorance, they shall give due and seasonable notice, that every such parent or master be summoned to the next court of magistrates, who are to proceed as they find cause, either to a greater fine, taking security for due conformity to the scope and intent of this law, or may take such children or apprentices from such parents or masters, and place them for years, boys till they come to the age of one and twenty, and girles till they come to the age of eighteen years, with others, who shall better educate and govern them, both for publick conveniency, and for the par-ticular good of the said children or apprentices.[3]

This statute reproduced almost verbatim the requirement of the laws of 1642 and 1650, that all children must be brought up in learning and labor, except that it omitted labor. The omission was not important, however, for we find in practice that the apprentices of the New Haven colony were taught "useful" trades in accordance with earlier custom. The "officers in publick trust" were instructed "to have" the same "vigilant eye over" parents and masters to see that the order was observed, and, where violations occurred, were to use the same means of enforcement. Children and apprentices whose education had been neglected, after their parents or masters had been warned and fined, were to be taken by the officers and apprenticed "with others who shall better educate and govern them." The New Haven law was more lenient than the Connecticut Code in that the penalty for the first offense was a warning, rather than a fine. "Three months after such warning," if the neglect had not been remedied, a fine of 10 shillings was imposed. "And lastly, if after the said warning, and the fines paid and levied," the neglect continued, "the magistrates . . . are to proceed either to a greater fine . . . or may take such

[3] Records of the Colony of New Haven, 583–84.

children or apprentices from such parents or masters," and bind them out.

In 1664 when the Connecticut and New Haven colonies were united the 1650 Code became operative for the whole province. Connecticut had now established throughout the colony the institution which Massachusetts had found so effective in providing elementary education for all children. The law ordered reading for all, and trade training for those not of independent living.

Later legislation shows the need of reenforcing the Act of 1650. In 1675, the Court "solemnly recommend" that the ministers instruct families, in which family worship and instruction of children were neglected, in their duty, and required "townsmen to inquire after such families and assist the ministry for the reformation and education of the children in good literature and the knowledge of the Scripture," according to the law.[4] It will be recalled that Massachusetts, at an early date, often delegated to the ministers the duty of catechising children. This order was not designed to relieve the town officers from their duty, however. It is probable that they made such an interpretation, and assumed that the ministers would do the work alone. At any rate, the town officers became so negligent that it was necessary in 1684 to impose upon them a fine of 20 shillings for each neglect.[5] In 1690, the Court "observing that notwithstanding the former orders made for the education of children and servants; there are many persons unable to read the English tongue," ordered "that the grand jurymen in each towne doe once in the year at least, vissit each famaly they suspect to neglect this order . . . and if they find such children and servants not taught as theire years are capable of, they shall return the names of the parents or masters of the sayd children so untaught to the next county court, where the sayd parents or masters shall be fyned twenty shillings." [6] An Act of 1702 further enjoined the grand jurymen in each town to be "very careful in seeing the education of children

---

[4] Conn. Col. Recs., II, 281.　　[5] *Ibid.*, III, 148.　　[6] *Ibid.*, IV, 30.

duly performed"; and grand jurymen and selectmen, as well as masters, were to be fined twenty shillings for each neglect. This Act definitely assigned to the ministers the duty of catechising.

So far we have considered the practice established by the 1650 Code, and subsequent legislation. The practice of apprenticeship antedated this legislation, however, and the records indicate that certain aspects of the educational requirement had been observed for some time. The earliest Connecticut records show the existence of the custom of teaching apprentices a "useful" trade. One of the earliest references to apprenticeship in Connecticut is contained in the record of a "Cort at Hartford, March 28, 1637," in which the master is "ordered to teach his servants in the trade of carpenter according to his promise." [7] Evidently in this instance the indenture had contained the master's promise to teach his apprentice a trade, but the master had neglected it. The apprentice, or his parent, or the town officers had then entered a complaint, which was followed by the Court order mentioned. From a New Haven record of the following year we learn that masters were occasionally required to give their apprentices a certain amount of "learning."

A Generall Court 25th of Feb. 1649: Charles Higginson is . . . to be with Thomas Fugill as apprentice unto the full end and tearme of nine years. The said Tho: Fugill is to find him what is convenient for him as a servant and to keepe him att schoole one yéare, or else to advantage him as much in his education as a years learning comes to.[8]

The curriculum of the school referred to is unknown, but it is probable that reading and writing, at least, were taught.

Records of a later date indicate that apprentices often received more than the rudiment required by law.

At a meeting of the Townsmen, Feb. 4, 1655. . . . Also an agreement made with William Edwards, Cooper, of Hartford. He is to take Simon Hillier, son of John Hillier, and keep him until he is 21 years of age,

---

[7] Public Records of the Colony of Connecticut, I, 8.
[8] Records of the Colony of New Haven, 30.

which will be completed and ended on the 25th day of Dec. 1665; he is
to learn him the trade of a cooper.[9]

In a Windsor indenture of 1727 the master promises "to
teach or cause the sd apprentice to be taught the art of Arithmatick to such a degree that he may be able to keep a book
well." [10]   Although the law demanded that children be taught
only reading in addition to the "capital laws," "the principles of religion," and a "useful" trade, many masters provided
instruction in reading, writing, and cyphering.   As in the
Massachusetts Bay colony, there was a growing demand for
a more complete elementary education, and it was provided
by the apprenticeship system long before it was required by
legislation.

For a complete account of the relationship that existed
between master and apprentice it is necessary to examine a
typical Connecticut indenture.   The indenture is the most
valuable record for this purpose, for it sums up and presents
in compact form the content of a great many separate records
from other sources.

This Indenture witnesseth that Jonathan Stoughton, son of Thomas
Stoughton of Windsor in the county of hartford and Coloney of Connecticut in new england, with his father's consent hath put him selfe an apprentice to Nathan day of the aboue sd windsor county and coloney:
blacksmith and white smith to Learn his art, trade or mystery after the
manner of an Apprentice to serue him until the sd Jonathan Stoughton
attaines the age of twenty-one years, during all which time the sd apprentice his master faithfully shall serue, his secrets keep, his Lawfull commands gladly obaye he shall not do any damage to his sd master nor
see it don by others without giueing notice thereof to his sd master.
he shall not waste his sd master's goods or Lend them unLawfully to
aney, he shall not commit fornication nor contract matrimony within
the sd terme. at cards, dice or any other unlawfull game he shall not
play whereby his sd master may suffer damage. he shall not absent
himself day nor night from his master's service without his leave. nor
haunt ale houses, Taverns or playhouses butt in all things behave himselfe as a faithfull apprentice ought to do during ye sd terme, and the sd
master shall do his utmost to teach and Instruct ye sd apprentice In

[9] Stiles, Ancient Windsor, I, 146.   [10] *Ibid.*, I, 442.

the boue mentioned blacksmith and white smiths trade and mistery and to teach or caus the sd apprentice to be Taught the art of Arithmatick to such a degree that he may be able to keep a book well, and provide for him meat, drink, apparel, washing and lodging and phisick in sickness and health suitable for such an apprentice during the sd terme, and att the end of sd terme the sd master shall furnish the sd apprentice with two good new suits of apparel boath wooling and lining for all parts of his body suitable for such an apprentice besids that apparel he carrieth with him and for the performance of all and every the sd covenants and agreement either of the sd parties bind themselves unto the other by these presents in witness whereof they have interchangeably put their hands and seals this first day of September in the year of our Lord god, 1727.[11]

The similarities with the practice revealed by the English and Massachusetts Bay indentures will be evident at once. With very few changes in phraseology the customary obligations were assumed by master and apprentice. The apprentice bound himself for the usual term — until the age of twenty-one,[12] promised to serve faithfully, keep his masters' secrets, obey his "lawful commands,"[13] protect his master from "damage . . . don by others," not absent himself by day or night from his master's service without his leave,[14] and

---

[11] Stiles, Ancient Windsor, I, 442.

[12] Records of the Colony of New Haven, 30.   Court record of 1639: "tearme of nine years."

Early Conn. Probate Records, I, 5.   Will of 1641 provides "yt my two children be sett forth in some Godly family for 6 or 7 years or more."

Pub. Recs. Col. of Conn., I, 222.   Court record of 1661: "until he is of the age of twenty-one years."

Stiles, Ancient Windsor, I, 146.   Town meeting minute, 1655: "until 21."

Pub. Recs. Col. of Conn., I, 112.   Court record, 1662: "until the age of 21."

Ibid., I, 516.   Will of 1689 provides "that the girls be bound until 18 years of age . . . and that Abraham be bound until 21 years of age."

[13] The revision of 1702 enacted "that whatsoever child or servant within this colony, upon complaint, shall be convicted of any stubborn or rebellious carriage against their parents or governors, any two assistants or justices are hereby authorized and empowered to commit such person or persons to the house of correction, there to remain under hard labor and severe punishment as long as they shall judge meet."

[14] As in Mass. Bay, runaways were punished by being compelled to serve extra time. An Act of 1644 provided that "Whereas many stubborn and refractory and discontented searvants and apprentices withdraw themselves from their

to observe proper moral conduct. The master, in accordance with his covenant, promised to provide meat, drink, apparel, "phisick," [15] and to teach the apprentice his trade, and in this instance, the rudiments of "Arithmatick."

RHODE ISLAND

The Rhode Island and Providence Plantations enacted no legislation comparable to the Massachusetts Bay Act of 1642 or the Connecticut Code of 1650. The practice of apprenticeship as carried on in these colonies was adopted by Rhode Island without colony or town action, and it served the same purposes. In the absence of legislation on the subject it may be assumed that all children were required to be brought up in "learning and labor," and if this were neglected such children were taken from their parents and bound out as apprentices. Apprentices who were neglected were taken from their masters and bound to others.

In order to learn a trade it was necessary to serve an apprenticeship. The apprenticeship system offered the only

masters services . . . it is ordered that whatsoever searvant or apprentice shall hereafter offend in this kynd, before their covenants or terme of searvice are expired, shall searve their said Masters as they shall be apprehended or retayned the treble terme, or threefold tyme of their absence in such kynd." (Pub. Recs. Col. of Conn., I, 105) This order was repeated in the 1650 Code, and in 1672.

Runaways were usually advertised and rewards offered for their apprehension. The Boston Gazette or Weekly Journal, Tues., July 11, 1749, contains the following : "Ran away from his Master Thomas Ivers Ropemaker of Stratford in Connecticut the 15th Day of April last, a Prentice Boy named Peter Hepbron, of about 17 years of Age had on when he went away a light colour'd Cloth Pea Jacket a blew Vest and strip'd Waistcoat and blew Camblet Breeches, and a Pair of Trowsers, wore a Wig or Cap, a lusty rugged Lad of a swarthy Complexion, with gray Eye. Whoever shall apprehend said Apprentice and shall secure him in any of his Majesty's Goals, so that his Master may have him again, shall receive the sum of twenty pounds old Tenor, and all necessary Charges paid by me Thomas Ivers."

See also Connecticut Journal, New Haven, Dec. 13, 1798; Sept. 4, 1799; Dec. 5, 1799.

[15] The parent-to-child relationship included the responsibility of the master to provide proper medical attention in case of sickness. A master of Hartford in 1655 was required by the town "to get his (the apprentice) scurf head cured." (Stiles, Ancient Windsor, I, 146)

means of becoming an artisan of any kind. If old enough a minor selected the calling he desired to follow, and bound himself, with his parent's consent, to a master; otherwise the parent decided it for him. This difference was always incorporated in the form of indenture or record; the former usually reads as follows: "I Henry Straight of Rhoad Island in New England of my owne free and voluntary will put myself an apprentice";[16] the latter type of apprenticeship may be observed in a record like the following: "Mercy Estance hath put . . . her Daughter Jerusa Sugars . . . to be an Apprentice . . . untill the said Child doe attaine to the full & just age of Eighteene yeares . . . said master . . . to learn the said Jerusa Sugars the art & mistry of a Tailor . . . & to learn her to Read Well."[17] Both were known as voluntary apprentices.

Poor-children and orphans were bound out by the town — boys until twenty-one, and girls until eighteen years of age — to masters who would bring them up properly. A Providence record of Nov. 26, 1662, indicates the form of procedure in such cases: "The Towne hath put . . . Daniell Comstock to William Carpenter to be an Apprentice untill the said Ladd be Twenty and one years of age."[18] The Overseers of the Poor were instructed to look about for "suitable" masters, and, if possible, place such children without expense to the town. If this could not be done, the town paid for the care and maintenance of its wards.

Council Meeting, Providence, Sept. 24, 1722. It is voted that Richard wickes shall have the sum of ten pounds allowed him out of the Towns treasury toward bringing up the Child: upon signeing an Indenture for

---

[16] Early Records of the Town of Portsmouth, 414. Indenture dated Dec. 24, 1667.

[17] Early Records of the Town of Providence, V, 17. Dated Jan. 11, 1708.

[18] *Ibid.*, III, 31.

Ibid., XII, 55. Providence, 1716.

Ibid., IX, 85. Providence, 1724. Girl bound until 18 years of age.

Early Records of the Town of Portsmouth, 430. Portsmouth, 1678. Boy for ten years.

Ibid., 432. Portsmouth, 1678. Girl for "ffifteene years."

the bringing up . . . untill the age of twenty one: It is . . . ordered that the overseers of the poor . . . signe an Indenture of sd Child to Richard Wickes. . . . The Childs name is John Blackstone Jr and he is to be Learned to Reade and brought up in the art of husbandry.[19]

Orphans with estates were bound out in the usual manner, and their masters were paid from the estate a sum agreed upon between the town and the masters.

The Town Councill (Feb. 4, 1695) have agreed with ye sd Nicholas Sheldon to take ye sd Daniel ffield an apprentice . . . the said Nicholas Sheldon to have 50s paid out of ye sd Zach: ffield (Daniel ffield's father) his Estate . . . & to learne sd Ladd to Reade & Rite.[20]

It is evident from these and similar records that the town required for the children whom it placed out a certain amount of education in addition to trade instruction.

The indenture with a few minor changes follows the model used by the Massachusetts Bay colony.

This Indenture witnesseth that I william Potter son of John Potter of Prouidence in the Colony of Rhoad Island and Prouidence plantations, (deceased) hath put himself and by these presents with the free and full Consent of his mother Jane Potter: Put himself an apprentis to Daniel Cook of the same Town and Colony aforesaid Joyner to Learn his Art After the manner of an apprentice to serue him the said Daniel Cook his Executors or administrators from the day of the date of these Presents untill he the said William Potter shall attaine and Com to the full age of twenty one yeares; dureing all which term the said Apprentis his said master faithfully shall serue his secrits Keepe his Lawful Commands Euery where obey: he shall do no Damage to his said master nor seene to be don of others without Giueing notis there of unto his said master he shall not wast his said masters Goods nor lend them unlawfully to any att Cards Dice or any unlawful Game he shall not Play where by his said master may haue damage in his own Goods or others he shall not Cummit fornication nor Contract Matrimony with in the said term; he shall not absent himself day nor night from his said masters seruis without his Leaue, Nor haunt aile Houses or Taverns: but in all things be haue himself as a faithfull apprentis ought to do dureing all the said term And I the said Daniel Cook do promise and Ingage for myself my Executors and administrators to Learn and Instruct my said Apprentis

[19] *Early Records of the Town of Providence,* XII, 40.   [20] *Ibid.,* X, 35.

William Potter In the trade mistry or art of a Joyner in the best manner that I Can within the said term; and also Instruct him in the trade of a House Carpenter as I haue oppertunity: and not put him to any other servis dureing the sd term without his Concent; and also Learn or Cause him to be Learned or taught to Reade English and wright and Cypher so far as to keepe a Booke: and to find and Prouide for him sufficient meate Drink apparrill Lodging and washing befitting an apprentis dureing all the said term: And when the said term is Expired which will be in the yeare of our Lord; one thousand seauen hundred and nineteene or twenty; then to sett him ffree: with as Good apparill in all Respects fit for his body throughout as he now is in at his first Entring into his seruis: the which apparill is perticuliorly named on the back side of this Indenture. for the true performance here of Each party binds themselues unto the other firmly by these presents. In witness where of they haue here unto Enter Changeable sett there hands and seals this twenty ninth day of march anno Domoni one thousand seauen hundred and sixteene. [21]

Master and apprentice bound themselves to fulfill the customary obligations during the usual term — "Until twenty-one years of age." [22]

Violations of covenant were punished by colony and town action. Masters who "put away" their apprentices, and apprentices who ran away without "license" or "sufficient" cause were punished in accordance with the provisions of the Providence Code of 1647.

Breach of Covenant is by this present Assembly, forbidden throwout the whole Colonie. . . .

And be it further enacted, that no person retayning a servant, shall putt their servant away, nor no person retayned shall depart from their

[21] Early Records of the Town of Providence, IX, 12.

[22] Similar obligations and terms appear in the following indentures, and town meeting minutes:
Early Recs. Town of Prov., II, 37. "Terme of Seauen Years." 1659.
Ibid., III, 31. "Twentye and one Year of age." 1662.
Ibid., V, 292. "fifteene yeares and a halfe." 1674.
Ibid., V, 146. "until 21 years old." 1696.
Ibid., V, 17. Girl, "to age of Eighteene yeares." 1708.
Ibid., XII, 40. "until the age of twenty one." 1722.
Ibid., IX, 85. Girl, "until eighteen years." 1724.
Early Recs. Town of Portsmouth, 412. Boy, "fowertene yeares." 1663.
Ibid., 430. Boy, "ten years." 1678.
Ibid., 432. Girl, "ffifteene years." 1678.

master, mistress, or dame, untill the end of the term covenanted for, unless it be for some reasonable and sufficient cause, witnessed before and allowed by the Head Officer or Officers of the Towne and three or foure able and discreet men of the Common Councill or Towne appointed thereto, under their hands in writing, for the discharge eyther of Master or Servant.

And be it enacted further, that that Master, Mistress, or Dame, that putts away their servant without sufficient cause, and so allowed with such a discharge, shall forfeit the sum of forty shillings; and if any servant departe from his or her Master, Mistress, or Dame's service, before the end of the Terme covenanted for, unless it be for some sufficient cause allowed of as before, or not serve according to the tenure of the promise or covenant, upon complaint unto the Head Officers of the Towne and their associates, the matter being fully proved, he shall be committed to Ward without Baile or Mainprize, untill by sufficient sureties he be bound to his Master, Mistress, or Dame, to perform the engagement.

Be it also enacted, by the authority abovesaid that he that shall retaine a Servant not lawfully dismissed and sett at liberty from his master, shall forfeit for every such offence five pounds which the Master may recover by an action of Debt.[23]

If the master neglected to provide sufficient "meat, drink, and lodging," the apprentice could obtain redress by appearing before the town authorities and lodging a complaint. An interesting case appears in the minute of "a Towne Cowncill held att Providence ye 13th day of April 1717:

Whereas William Dalie saruant of Joseph Dalie appeared before this Councill with *a Complaint against his sd master for want of Cloathing and Lodging* for the which Complaint ye sd saruant or Apprentis hath bin placed for sum time past with Samuel Bates: And the Councill haueing Considered ye premises haue ordered as followeth that ye sd Lad shall abide with ye sd Samuel Bates untill his sd master shall prouide such apparil as Major ffenner shall approue of to be Conveniant for sd apprentis the which sd Cloathing sd Joseph Dalie is to bring to major ffenners house and then ye sd Major ffenner If he approueth of them to be sufficient to send a few lines to Samuel Bates to bring sd Lad to his house: and sd Joseph Dalie to be Accountable to sd Bates for his trouble att ye discression of sd major fenner.[24]

[23] Records of the Colony of Rhode Island and Providence Plantations, I, 182. Code of Laws for the Province of Providence, 1647, drawn up at a General Court of Election held at Portsmouth. (See 5 Eliz. 4)

[24] Early Recs. Town of Providence, XII, 56.

The apprentice was taken away from his master, and placed with another master who provided for him. In the meantime his former master was ordered to provide "such apparil as Major ffenner (one of the town officials) shall approue," and bring it to "major ffenners house." If it were approved the master could regain his apprentice by paying for his maintenance during the time he lived with the new master. The town fixed the charges "att ye discression" of its officer.

All apprentices whether voluntary or placed out by the town because of poverty, lack of a guardian, or neglect of education, received a more or less complete elementary education. In some cases it included only "to Reade"; [25] this was the usual provision for girls, in accordance with earlier custom. In others the master was obliged to teach his apprentice "to Reade & Rite." [26] Finally, as the demand became more widespread, masters were required to teach their apprentices "to Reade English and wright and Cypher." [27]

---

[25] Early Recs. Town of Providence, XII, 40. Town order, 1722, for poor boy.
Ibid., V, 17. Girl, "to read well." 1708.
Ibid., IX, 5. Girl, "to Read." 1713.
Ibid., IX, 85. Girl, "to Reade English." 1724.
[26] Early Recs. Town of Providence, X, 35. 1695.
Ibid., V, 146. "to read & write." 1696.
Ibid., XII, 55. "to write & Reade." 1716.
[27] Early Recs. Town of Providence, IX, 5. 1713.

CHAPTER V

THE PRACTICE OF APPRENTICESHIP IN THE PROVINCE OF NEW YORK AS REVEALED BY POOR–LAWS

THE first provision made for education in the Province of New York was the extension of the educational requirements of the apprenticeship system. This was contained in the Duke of York's Laws of 1665, drawn up shortly after the English occupation.

The Constables and Overseers are strictly required frequently to Admonish the Inhabitants of Instructing their Children and Servants in Matters of Religion and the Lawes of the Country, And that Parents and Masters do bring up their Children and Apprentices in some honest and Lawful Calling Labour or Employment.[1]

From the tenor of this requirement, and from the fact that the entire Code of 1665 had been "collected out of the several laws now in force in his Majesty's American colonies and plantations," it is evident that the delegates to the convention at Hempstead had before them the Massachusetts Bay Act of 1642. Each law emphasized the principle that all children must be brought up in learning and labor. The 1665 Code provided for all "children and apprentices," and therefore included both voluntary apprentices and those bound out by public authority, although it did not designate each class separately.

The first reference to apprenticeship as a method of poor-relief appears in a statute enacted by the Dongan Assembly of Nov. 1, 1683, entitled "An Act for Defraying of the publique and necessary Charge of each respective Citty, towne

[1] Col. Laws of N. Y., I, 26.

and County throughout this Province & for maintaining
the poore & preventing vagabonds." This act provided

> Thatt annually . . . there shall bee elected a certaine number out of
> each respective Citty Towne and County throughout this Province . . .
> which . . . shall have power & authority to make an assessment or cer-
> taine Rate . . . for defraying of all the publique and necessary charges
> of each respective place above menconed.
> And farther Whereas itt is the Custome & practice of his Majestys
> Realm of England, and all the adjacent Colonys in America that every
> respective County Citty towne parrish & precinct doth take care & pro-
> vide for the poor who do inhabit in their respective precincts aforesaid.
> Therefor itt is Enacted by the authority aforesaid thatt for the time
> to come the respective Commissioners of every County, Citty, Towne
> parish & Precinct aforesaid shall make provision for the maintenance
> support of their poor respectively.[2]

The Act of 1683 was virtually repealed by "An Act for
Defraying the Publick and necessary Charge throughout
this Province, and for maintaining the Poor and Preventing
Vagabonds" passed May 13, 1691, which made the support
of the poor a town charge only.[3] Furthermore it limited
the "certaine number" to "two freeholders." Neither Act
named these officers, but Overseers of the Poor were mentioned in the Code of 1665. The "custome" of England required that the children of poor parents be placed out as
apprentices by the Overseers of the Poor, or Church Wardens.
But it was not until 1693 that Church Wardens were definitely mentioned in connection with poor-relief. In that
year, "An Act for Settling a Ministry and Raising a Maintenance for them in the city of New York, County of Richmond, Westchester, and Queens County," provided

> That the respective Justices of Every City County aforesaid or any
> two of them Shall every year issue out their warrants to the constables
> to summon the ffreeholders of every City County and Precinct aforesaid
> together on the 2d Tuesday in January for the chusing of *ten Vistry men
> and two Church Wardens* and the said Justices and Vistry men or the
> major part of them are hereby empowered . . . to lay a reasonable Tax

---

[2] Col. Laws of N. Y., I, 132.
[3] *Ibid.*, I, 237. Repeated May 11, 1697, and May 20, 1708.

on the respective City County parish or precinct *for the Maintenance of the Minister and Poor* of their respective places.[4]

Although this Act did not assign to the Church Wardens the duty of Overseers of the Poor in regard to the apprenticing of poor-children, it may be assumed that they exercised that function in cooperation with the Overseers.

The records indicate that the Church Wardens were actually binding out poor-children, In accordance with the English custom, shortly after the Act mentioned. In the minutes of "a Court of Record held at the City Hall on Tuesday the 13th day of January Anno Dom. 1719," we read

> Ordered that the Church Wardens Inspect in what Condition the Widow and Children of Thomas Gregson are in at the Bowery & if they find the Children Objects of Charity that they Relieve them at their discretions or put them out Apprentice for a term of Years.[5]

The same Court of Record, on June 30, 1719, issued the following order:

> Ordered that the Church Wardens put Susannah Maria Beyer a poor Child Without any parents, or Relations in this City Aged about Nine years Apprentice unto Obadiah Hunt & Susannah his wife for the Term of Nine Years the Master & Mistress to Maintain with Apparell Meat Drink washing & Lodging & teach her Housewifery.[6]

A large number of similar records appears in the Mayor's Court Minutes.[7]

In the practice of poor-law apprenticeship the child of poor parents was placed with a master whose qualifications were acceptable to the Overseers of the Poor or Church Wardens, and who was willing to take an apprentice. It

[4] Col. Laws of N. Y., I, 328. Also Laws of N. Y. Bradford edition of 1694, 72.

[5] Minutes of Mayors Court, Jan. 1717 to June 1721, Vol. II. Manuscript folio. Pages not numbered. Items entered chronologically.

[6] Minutes of Mayors Court, Jan. 1717 to June 1721, Vol. II.

[7] Minutes of Mayors Court, Jan. 1717 to June 1721, Vol. II. Entries under dates: Oct. 27, 1719; May 24, 1720; Mar. 20, 1721.

Minutes of Mayors Court, Jan. 26, 1724 to June 1729. Entries under dates: Dec. 13, 1726; Mar. 12, 1727; Feb. 25, 1729; Oct. 22, 1729; Dec. 24, 1729.

is hardly probable that a master was obliged to accept an apprentice if he did not want one. The Overseers were required by law "to take Order, from time to time . . . to raise a competent Sum of Money, yearly, to purchase proper materials for the Poor to work on; for the necessary relief of such poor People as are not able to work; *and for putting out poor Children Apprentices.*" [8] Although the records of pauper-apprenticeship do not refer to this practice, it is probable that the New England custom obtained, of making an agreement with the prospective master to take an apprentice for a certain sum of money to be paid out of public funds.

The boy, if old enough to know, may have been consulted in regard to the trade he preferred to learn, and the Overseers or Church Wardens may have placed him with a master of that trade. Otherwise, he had no choice in the matter, and was obliged to serve the master to whom he was bound by the public officers. Many such masters must have been men of uncertain temper, or otherwise undesirable as foster parents, and, in consequence, their apprentices found life with them more or less unendurable at times. But the law did not take this into consideration, except where masters were unduly abusive and cruel. Sometimes, however, a pauper-apprentice was rescued from a long term of service to a stranger, when a relative came forward and offered to provide for him. In that event the case was taken to court, and the apprentice was freed from his master, and bound to his relative. A Quarter Sessions Court record of 1739 illustrates such a case:

Stephen Wood an Infant Aged about twelve years who was bound out Apprentice to John Deffer of the City of New York Cordwainer untill he attain the Age of Twenty one years whereas the said John Deffer & Gertie Wood the Mother of the said Stephen Wood have prayed the Court that the said Stephen Wood be discharged from the said Apprenticeship, an Uncle of the said Stephen Wood promising to undertake to provide for the said Stephen Wood & to educate him in Husbandry.

[8] Poor laws of 1747, 1754, 1763, 1768, 1772. This "Sum of Money" is the assessment or "certaine Rate" mentioned in the Act of Nov. 1, 1683.

It is therefore orderd that the said Stephen Wood be discharged from the said Apprenticeship.[9]

If a father deserted his family,[10] or was committed to jail, his children were treated as poor children, and bound out accordingly. "Att a Common Councill held att the Citty Hall of the Said Citty on the 27th day of Feb. 1693," the Overseers of the Poor were ordered to place out the children of a prisoner. The Council record follows.

Pursuant to an Order of ye Govr. and Council bearing Date the fifteenth Instant upon Petition of John L. Roux now a Prisoner in this City and referring the Same to the Mayor and Aldermen of the Said City that they Consider to Supply the Necessities of ye Prisoner's wife and children or to give an Account next Thursday unto the Council of their Reasons to the Contrary. Ordered that the Overseers of the Poor doe put the Children of the Said Petitioner in some Good Reputable Families for their Subsistence dureing his Imprisonment.[11]

Either the Church Wardens were not yet acting as Overseers, or the Court, at its discretion, discriminated between the two classes of officials in assigning certain tasks. A record of 1725, however, contains the definite assignment of the Church Wardens to a similar duty.

Att a Court of Record held at the City Hall of the said City on Tuesday the 20th day of July Anno Dom. 1725.

Ordered the Church Wardens do provide for or put out for a Term of years in the best Manner they can Joseph Byng an Infant aged Eighteen Months or thereabouts son of Thomas Byng Feltmaker who is committed to the Common Gaol of the City for the Murder of his wife Martha.[12]

[9] Records of the Court of Quarter Sessions & of the Court of Sessions, May 1722 to Nov. 1742. Manuscript folio. Pages not numbered. Items entered chronologically.

[10] Minutes of Mayors Court, Jan. 26, 1724 to June 1729. "Att a Court of Record held at the City Hall of the Said City on Tuesday the first day of July Anno Dom. 1729. Whereas William Lane late of this City Victualler has privately withdrawn himself and left three Male Children very Young without anything to subsist them unless taken care of must perish. It is therefore Orderd that the Church Wardens do take Care of & provide for the subsistence of the said Children till such time as they Can put them out Apprentice till they attain the Age of one & twenty years."

[11] Minutes of the Common Council of the City of New York, I, 348.

[12] Minutes of Mayors Court, Jan. 26, 1724 to June 1729.

Orphans without estates were, in effect, poor children and were taken care of through the apprenticeship system. The administrators of estates belonging to minors were held strictly accountable for the improvement of such estates. Under the title "Orphants," in the Duke of York's Law of 1665, it was enacted

That all Persons who now have or shall have any Estate of Goods, Chattles or Lands, in their possession, belonging to any that are under age shall exhibite an Inventory and Accompts of that said Estate within three Moneths next after Publication of this Law, to the respective Courts of Sessions where such Estate shall be and afterwards yearly . . . and if any good Improvement hath not been made of the Estate . . . it shall be removed into the hands of some other able and discreet Person or Persons as the Court shall appoint.[13]

The maintenance and education of orphans were provided for in "An Act for the Supervising Intestates Estates, and regulating the Probate of Wills and granting Letters of Administration," of Nov. 11, 1692, which ordered

If the said Intestate did leave only Orphans behind him and has no Relations or Kindred who will administer upon the said Intestates Estate, then the Supervisor of each respective County delegated as aforesaid, shall only have the Administration and Care of the said Intestates Estate and the same shall secure, as aforesaid, for the Use, Benefit, and Behoof of the said Orphans, and not otherwise; And the said Intestates Estate, so inventoried as aforesaid, shall cause to be well secured, and improved to the best Advantage for the behoof of the said Orphans, until they marry or come to the Age of One and Twenty Years. And that *he shall likewise take effectual care for the Educating and Instructing of the said Orphans in the Holy Protestant Religion*, and they shall be honestly maintained according to the Capacity of the said Intestates Estate.[14]

If it were found that the estate were inadequate for the maintenance and education of such children, they became

[13] East Hampton Book of Laws, June ye 24th 1665; or N. Y. Province Laws, Duke of York, 1665, 375.

[14] Laws of N. Y., 1691–1751, 14. (Parker)
Laws of N. Y., 1691–1773, 292. (Gaine) An Act of Nov. 24, 1750 extended the Act of 1692 to Orange County.
Ibid., 707. An Act of Mar. 24, 1772 extended the 1692 Act to Tryon, Charlotte, Cumberland, and Gloucester counties.

town charges, and as such were taken by the Overseers or Church Wardens, and apprenticed to persons who would provide for them.[15]

"Att a Common Council held at the City Hall of the said City on Wed. 31st day of March Anno Dom. 1736," the Church Wardens were definitely appointed Overseers of the Poor for the City of New York. As we have seen, they had been serving in that office for some time. The enactment follows:

And the Church Wardens of this City be appointed Overseers of the Poor and that they have the Direction and providing of necessary supplys of Provisions for the said Workhouse and poorhouse out of the fund for the Maintenance of the Minister and poor, etc. . . . That such parish children as may be hereafter sent to the poorhouse for Maintainance, that Care be taken by the Masters thereof (by the Directions of the Church Wardens and Overseers of the Poor) that they be religiously educated and taught to read, write and cast account; and employed in spinning, in spinning wool, Thread, Knitting, Sewing or other Labour most suitable to their Genius in order to qualify them to be put out apprentices.[16]

The Church Wardens continued to serve in this capacity until "An Act for the Settlement and Relief of the Poor," passed April 17, 1784, abolished their office. This general statute ordered

That the Office of Church Wardens, Vestrymen for overseeing, relieving or settling the Poor becoming a Public charge, heretofore established or used in the City of New York, and Queens, Richmond and Westchester Counties be and the same offices hereby respectively are annulled and abolished; and at all times hereafter there shall be annually elected in and for the City and County of New York two Overseers of the Poor for each respective Ward, who with the Mayor, Recorder and Alderman of the said City and County shall exercise all the Powers and authorities heretofore Appertaining to the Offices of Vestrymen of the said City, with respect to the overseeing, relieving, or settling the Poor, and binding out or placing of Apprentices.[17]

[15] See page 68.
[16] Minutes, Common Council, City of N. Y., IV, 309–310.
[17] Laws of N. Y., 1784, 46. (Holt)

This Act of abolishment reveals the fact that the Church Wardens had been administering poor-relief throughout the more important counties of the Province of New York.

During the later colonial period there were few general laws concerning the apprenticing of poor-children. The administration of poor-relief was left almost entirely to the various counties, manors, parishes, and towns. It was recognised by the General Assembly that one law could not be successfully applied everywhere. Consequently it enacted separate laws for the various subdivisions of the province.[18] Although no absolute uniformity characterised these Acts, the same general scheme of administering poor-relief bound them together. Each subdivision was permitted "to chuse and elect . . . so many Persons to be Overseers of the Poor, as the Majority of Freeholders and Inhabitants of such Town, Manor, and Precinct, then present, shall judge necessary," [19] and these Overseers were to proceed in the manner prescribed by the earliest poor-laws. No definite number of Overseers was designated. A general "Act for the Settlement and Relief of the Poor," of April 17, 1784, ordered that "at all times there shall be annually elected in and for

---

[18] "An Act for the Relief of the Poor in the County of Suffolk." Passed Nov. 25, 1747. (Laws of N.Y., 1691–1751, 404. Parker.)

"An Act for the Relief of the Poor in Dutchess County, to enable the Inhabitants of the several Precincts thereof, to elect Overseers of the Poor and to ascertain the Places of their respective Meetings." Passed Dec. 7, 1754. (Laws of N. Y., 1691–1773, 343. Gaine.) Repeated April 1, 1775 (Laws of N. Y., Jan.–Apr., 1775, 121).

"An Act for the Relief of the Poor in the Manor of Cortlandt, in the County of Westchester." Passed Dec. 13, 1763. (Laws of N. Y., 1691–1773, 438. Gaine.)

"An Act or the Relief of the Poor in the Counties of Ulster and Orange, and to enable the Freeholders and Inhabitants of the several Towns and Precincts thereof to elect Overseers of the Poor at their annual Meetings." Passed Dec. 31, 1768. (Col. Laws of N. Y., IV, 1060.)

"An Act to enable the Justices, Church Wardens and Vestry of the Parish of Westchester in the County of Westchester, to raise a Sum not exceeding five hundred pounds, for the Purposes therein mentioned." Passed Feb. 26, 1772. (Laws of N. Y., 1691–1773, 643. Gaine.)

"An Act for the Relief of the Poor in the County of Albany." Passed Mar. 8, 1773. (Laws of N. Y., 1691–1773, 799. Gaine.)

[19] "An Act for the Relief of the Poor in the County of Suffolk," 1747.

the City and County of New York two Overseers of the Poor for each respective Ward." [20]

Although each separate Act mentioned in the preceding paragraph was designed to meet the needs of the respective localities in regard to the general administration of poor-relief, the mode of procedure in dealing with poor-children remained constant. Each Act repeated the following order:

> said Overseers, by and with the Consent of two or more Justices of the Peace, are hereby impowered to bind Apprentices all such Children whose Parents, shall not by the Overseers and Justices aforesaid, be thought able to keep and maintain them, where they the said Overseers. and Justices as aforesaid, shall see convenient until such Male Child come to the age of Twenty-one Years, and such Female Child to the Age of Eighteen.

This was "the Custome & practice of his Majestys Realm in England, and all adjacent Colonys in America," mentioned in the enactment of the Dongan Assembly of Nov. 1, 1683

[20] Laws of N. Y., 1784, 46.   Holt.

CHAPTER VI

APPRENTICESHIP AND APPRENTICESHIP EDUCA-
TION IN THE PROVINCE OF NEW YORK AS
REVEALED BY LEGISLATION, COURT ORDERS,
ETC.

WHEN a master took an apprentice he was required by law to enter into an agreement or contract with the apprentice containing the promises or covenants that should govern their relations to each other. Then he must appear before the town authorities, and register the contract or indenture. The terms of the indenture were copied in a book kept for this purpose, and so became a public record.[1] Public enrollment of apprentices was insisted upon at a very early date in England, and was the custom in the New England colonies. Although the law of the mother-country obtained in the Province of New York from the date of occupation, the Common Council of the City of New York evidently found it necessary to remind the inhabitants of this requirement. It is probable that a number of cases of neglect had occurred. At any rate the following law was enacted:

---

[1] Earliest book is entitled "Citty of N. Yorke Indentures of Apprenticeship begun February 19, 1694 and ends Jan. ye 29th 1707." This is a manuscript folio volume preserved at the City Hall of New York City.

Another book of this character is entitled "Indentures Oct. 2, 1718 to Aug. 7, 1727." This is "Liber 29" which originally belonged to the Hall of Records of New York City. It is now in the library of the New York Historical Society.

A Common Council Act of Oct. 27, 1727 "Ordered the Mayor Issue his Warrant to the Treasurer to pay unto William Sharpes Town Clerk of this City ... the sum of fourteen pounds Nine Shillings and three pence Current Money of New York in full of half a Years Sallary due and Ending the fourteenth day of this Instant October, for Pens, Ink and Paper for one Year due and Ending the same time, *for a Book for Recording Indentures of Apprenticeship.* . . ." (Min. Com. Coun. City of N. Y., III, 423)

Att a Common Council held att the Citty Hall of the said Citty on Wensday the 16th day of January Anno Dom 1694.

Ordered that Noe Merchant handy Craft Tradesman Shall take Any Prentice to teach or instruct them in their Trade or Calling without being bound by Indentures before the Mayor Recorder or Any one of ye Aldermen of the Said Citty and Registered in the Town Clerkes Office and not for a Less Term than four Years; and att the Expiration of the Indentures the said Apprentice Shall be made Free of the Said Citty by his Said Master if he have well and truely Served him; and that the Clerke have for Registering each Indenture of Apprenticeship as Aforesaid the Sum of three Shillings to be paid by the Master of such Apprentice bound as Aforesaid.[2]

Every freeman, in "The Oath of a Freeman of the City of New York," was required to take the following oath: "YE SHALL SWEAR that . . . within the first year ye Shall Cause him (the apprentice) to be Enrolled or Else pay such fine as Shall be reasonably Imposed upon you for Omitting the same." [3]

This Act applied to poor-law apprentices as well as to voluntary apprentices. It will be recalled that the Duke of York's Laws "strictly required . . . that Parents and Masters do bring up their children and Apprentices in some honest and Lawful Calling Labour or Employment." And the records indicate that, in every case, Overseers of the Poor and

---

[2] Min. Com. Coun. City of N. Y., I, 373–74.

This Act was repeated at the following Common Councils: Nov. 19, 1695 (*Ibid.*, I, 388); Dec. 10, 1695 (*Ibid.*, I, 393); Nov. 23, 1697 (*Ibid.*, II, 22); Dec. 23, 1701 (*Ibid.*, II, 184); Feb. 15, 1702 (*Ibid.*, II, 223); Dec. 21, 1706 (*Ibid.*, II, 314); Mar. 7, 1711 (*Ibid.*, III, 3); Mar. 28, 1707 (Ordinances of the City of N. Y., 1707, 11); May 28, 1712 (Min. Com. Coun. City of N. Y., III, 3).

[3] Min. Com. Coun. City of N. Y., III, 392. Sept. 1, 1726. "THE OATH OF A FREEMAN OF THE CITY OF NEW YORK YE SHALL SWEAR that Ye Shall be good and true to our sovereign Lord King George. . . . The Franchises and Customs (of this city) Ye Shall Maintain. . . . Ye shall take no Apprentice for a less Term than for seven Years without fraud or deceit, and within the first year ye Shall Cause him to be Enrolled or Else pay such fine as Shall be reasonable Imposed upon you for Omitting the same, and after his Term Ends ye Shall make him free of this City if he have well and truly served you. . . . All these Points and Articles ye Shall well and truly keep According to the Laws and Customs of this City. So help you God." (Compare the Oath of Freemen of 1275, Chapter I, p. 2. Phraseology almost identical.)

Church Wardens bound out poor-children to some "Merchant or handy Craft Tradesman." Many poor girls were, of course, bound out to "Dames," but these women promised to teach their apprentices some "useful" occupation.

It will be noted that the Order of 1694 did not mention a fine as the penalty for non-compliance with the registration requirements. Complaints of violations were heard before the Mayor's Court, which usually freed the apprentices concerned. Such a case came before "a Court of Record held at the City Hall of the said City on Tuesday the first day of June Anno Dom. 1725," which decreed that "John Aspinwall Apprentice to Jde Meyer Shoemaker is discharged from his Apprenticeship his Indentures not being Acknowledged, made or Registered According to the Laws of this Corporation." [4]

The law also required a registration fee to be paid by the master upon enrolling an indenture. This practice dates from the thirteenth century in England. We find its counter-part in the early gild and municipal requirement of an entry fee. The available records of the New England colonies do not indicate whether such a requirement was in force there.

The usual term of apprenticeship, according to English legislation, was seven years, and it must not be completed until the apprentice was twenty-one years of age. In the Province of New York, however, the Common Council Act of 1694 permitted four-year terms, which action was, in effect, an annulment of the law of the mother-country. Such a law also operated in contravention to the primary purpose of the apprenticeship system, the production of skilled craftsmen. But early in the next century it was recognised by the city authorities that the four-year term was inadequate; the average apprentice could not successfully learn a trade in so short a period. "Att a Common Council held at the City Hall of the said City on Tuesday the 30th day of October, Anno Dom 1711," the earlier law was repealed,

[4] Minutes of Mayors Court, Jan. 26, 1724, to June, 1729.

and the time-honored seven-year term insisted upon. The Act follows:

Forasmuch as Great Inconveniencys have Arisen by Apprentices serving but four years by Reason whereof they are seldom Masters of their Trades for remedy whereof Be it Ordained by the Mayor Recorder Aldermen and assistants of the City of New York convened in Common Council and it is hereby Ordained by the Authority of the same that from henceforth no Merchant Shopkeeper or Handy Craft Tradesman Shall take any Apprentice to teach or Instruct In their trade or Calling without being bound by an Indenture before the Mayor Recorder or any one of the Aldermen of the said City and Registered in the Town Clerks Office and *not for a less Term than seaven years;* and at the Expiration of the said Indenture the said Apprentice shall be made free of the said City by the Master if he have well and truely served him and the Clerk Shall have for Registering each Indenture of Apprenticeship the Sum of three Shillings to be paid by the Master of such Apprentice bound as aforesaid and that all Indentures of Apprenticeship hereafter to be made within this City Contrary to the true Intent and Meaning hereof shall be void and of None Effect; any former Law of this Corporation to the Contrary hereof in any wise Notwithstanding.[5]

Furthermore all masters were required, in "The Oath of Freemen," to swear that "Ye shall take no apprentice for a less Term than for seven years."[6]   Not only were the four-year apprentices "seldom Masters of their Trades," but, in the phraseology of a similar Boston Act of 1660, they were unable "att the expiration of their Apprenticeship to take charge of others for government and manuall instruction in their occupation which, if not timely amended, threatens the welfare of this Town."[7]

Although girl-apprentices were not referred to in this Order, we know that they were required to serve until eighteen years of age or until they were married. This is borne out by the evidence of the indentures of apprenticeship, which will be considered in a later chapter, the Mayor's

[5] Min. Com. Coun. City of N. Y., II, 454–55.
Repeated Dec. 1, 1719 (*Ibid.*, II, 467); Sept. 1, 1726 (*Ibid.*, II, 475).
[6] Min. Com. Coun. City of N. Y., III, 392.   Sept. 1, 1726.
[7] Boston Records, II, 157.

Court Minutes referred to above,[8] and the Poor Laws of 1747, 1754, 1763, 1768, 1772, 1773, 1775.[9] A similar requirement had been in force for some time in the New England colonies.

Naturally during a period of seven years, at least, misunderstandings and actual conflicts arose between master and apprentice. Custom, and the parent-to-child relationship permitted masters to chastise unruly apprentices but, as in New England, the public authorities preferred to deal with cases of incorrigibility. Masters might complain to the Overseers, and these officers were empowered to administer the punishment provided by law. Such punishment usually consisted of a whipping. The Duke of York's Laws (1665) contained the following enactment on this point:

> If any Children or Servants become rude Stubborne or unruly refusing to hearken to the voice of their Parents or Masters the Constable and Overseers (where no Justice of the Peace shall happen to dwell within ten miles of the said Town or Parish) have power upon the complaint of their Parents or Masters to call before them such Offender, and to Inflict such Corporall punishment as the merrit of their fact in their Judgment shall deserve, not exceeding ten Stripes, provided that such children and Servants be of Sixteen years of age.[10]

An interesting record of two centuries later indicates that the master was permitted to whip an apprentice "severely." Such punishment was justifiable on the ground that the "master was bound to preserve the same course towards his apprentice as a father towards his son." An article in the "New York and Richmond County Free Press, Dec. 21, 1833, presents the public attitude toward the matter. The item follows:

"Master and Apprentice"

The following is the substance of a trial which took place in New York on Tuesday week, in reference to a question which from time to time, causes considerable discussion as to the control which masters

---

[8] Page 68, notes 6 and 7.　　　　[9] Page 73, note 18.
[10] Col. Laws of N. Y., I, 26.

possess over apprentices, and the relative position in which they stand toward each other.   The Commercial Advertiser of Wednesday says —

In the sessions a cause was tried which involved a principle of much interest to the community. Levi Chapman, a pocket-book maker, doing an extensive business in William street, was placed on trial for severely whipping an apprentice, named Isaac Wilson, a boy about 17 years of age, who had lived with the defendant two or three years.

(A lengthy account of the evidence follows.)

It was due to the whole community that the case should be made public, and that apprentices should be made to understand their duties. The Recorder charged the Jury that a master was bound to preserve the same course towards his apprentice, as a father towards his son — that in the present the disobedience and threats of the apprentice were highly reprehensible; and that, for himself, if his own son had pursued a course as the boy Wilson had done, he should have chastised and brought him to obedience.[11]

But the colonists made a distinction between "severely whipping," and "unreasonable Correcting." If an apprentice were unduly punished his complaint might be taken to court, and, if it were proved, he was discharged from his apprenticeship.   The Code of 1665 provided

If any Masters or Dames shall Tyrannically and Cruelly abuse their Servants, upon complaint made by the Servant to the Constable and Overseers, they shall take Speedy redress therein, by Admonishing the Master or Dame not to provoke their Servants, And upon the Servants Second Complaint, of the like usage, It shall be lawful for the Constable and Overseers to protect and Sustaine such Servants in their Houses till due Order be taken for their Reliefe in the ensuing Sessions provided that due Notice thereof be Speedily given to Such Masters or Dames, and the Cause why such Servants are protected and Sustained, and in Case any Master or Dame by such Tyranny and Cruelty, and not Casually, shall smite out the Eye or Tooth of Any such Servant after due proof made shall be sett free from their Service, And have a further allowance and recompence as the Court of Sessions shall judge meet.[12]

[11] New York and Richmond County Free Press, Dec. 21, 1833.

[12] Col. Laws of N. Y., I, 48.

Repeated by Act of Oct. 24, 1684 (*Ibid.*, I, 157); and Act of Dec. 19 ,1766: "may be relieved and discharged for Missusage, Refusal of Necessaries Cruelty or Ill treatment in the manner Apprentices are relievable in England for any of the Causes aforesaid." (*Ibid.*, IV, 924.)   Until such cases were settled the Overseers were often obliged to "Sustaine such Servants in their Houses."

The Minutes of the Mayor's Court, and the Records of the Court of Quarter Sessions contain many records of the enforcement of this legislation.   At a "Court of Record of the Citty, holden att the Citty Hall within the Citty, the 13th day of May 1681," a case of violation was brought up, and the master was admonished according to the law.   The decree follows:

> Deft pleades that ye Servt was his Sonne & by reason of ye plts ill usage towards him by unreasonable Correction he would not live with him & therefore came to the Deft his father where he now is.   Mr. Beekeman informed ye Court of ye matter haveing been examined before him. The Court Orders that ye Servt return to his Mastr & serve his time agreed on according to Indenture if ye plt for ye future shall give him any undue & unreasonable Correction or usage then ye Servt to be freed. ye plt to paie Costs.[13]

In another instance the apprentice was actually freed from his master.   The record follows:

> Att a Court of General Quarter Sessions of the Peace held for the City and County of New York at the City Hall on Wednesday the fourth day May Anno Dom. 1731.
> Upon Complaint of Samuell Magee of the City of New York Cordwainer that Thomas Hall of the said City Cordwainer hath several times very immoderately corrected his son Alexander Magee an Apprentice to the said Thomas Hall without just occasion & prayeth the Court that his said son Alexander Magee be discharged from his Apprenticeship for the causes aforesd, & upon hearing of the Parties & seeing the marks upon the head, Arm and body of the said Alexander Magee of the said immoderate Correcting it is Ordered by the said Court that the said Alexander Magee is hereby discharged from his said Apprenticeship.[14]

[13] Mayors Court, Rough Minutes, Nov. 1680 to Oct. 1683.   Manuscript folio volume.   Pages not numbered.   Items entered chronologically.

[14] Records of the Court of Quarter Sessions & of the Court of Sessions, May 1722 to Nov. 1742.   Manuscript folio volume.   Pages not numbered.

Ibid., Feb. 5, 1725: "upon hearing of a Complaint of Mary Anderson Widow agt Benjamin Bake Cordwainer for unreasonable Correcting her Daughter Margaret his Apprentice aged about Eleven years & very often Immoderately Correcting her & not allowing her reasonable time to rest several times in the Night time it is Ordered by the Court for the Causes aforseaid that the said Margaret Anderson by the Court be discharged from her said Apprenticeship."

Minutes of Mayors Court, Jan. 26, 1724 to June 1729.   July 19, 1726: boy discharged from his apprenticeship on complaint against his master "for Immoderately Correcting him."

Discharged apprentices were bound out to other masters, in compliance with the law which required that all children not of independent estate be brought up in some "honest lawful" calling.

The same legislation made provision for "Refusal of Necessaries," and "after due proof made," apprentices who were denied "sufficient meat, drink and lodging," were set free. A case in point appears in a Long Island record of Nov. 2, 1738.

> Queens County YSs Whereas Caleb Cornall Joseph Thorne Thomas Cornall Hennery Allyn four of his Majestys Justices of the Peace Whereof one is of ye Quorum for ye County afore Said having heard and Examined ye Matter in Differance between Joseph Dodge an apprentice to Jeremiah Dodge hath not allowed his Apprintice Sufficient Meat We Do therefore for ye Cause afore said Discharge ye Said Joseph Dodge from his said Apprentice ship and Do hereby Under our Respective hands and Seals pronounce and Declare that ye Said Joseph Dodge is Discharged from his being any Longer an Apprintice to his said Master. As Witness our hands and Seals this 2th day of November 1738.[15]

Apprentices who ran away from their masters were, if apprehended and brought back, obliged to serve "double the time of such their absence." Under the title "Fugitives," the Duke of York's Laws contained the following Order:

> Every Apprentice and Servant that shall depart or absent themselves from their Master or Dame without leave first obtained shall be Adjudged by the Court to double the time of such their absence by future Service over and above other Damage and Cost which the Master or Dame shall Sustain by such unlawful departure.[16]

If necessary, in order to bring back runaways, "Every Justice of the Peace or any Constable with two Overseers where no Justice is at hand," had the "power to press Men, Horses, Boats, or Pinnaces, at Publique Charge, to pursue such persons both by Sea and Land and to bring them back by force of Armes."[17] It is doubtful whether such extreme

---

[15] Recs. of the Towns of North and South Hempstead, Long Island, III, 219.
[16] Col. Laws of N. Y., I, 36. Repeated Oct. 22, 1684 (*Ibid.*, I, 147).
[17] *Ibid.*, I, 48.

means were often employed. Usually, at a later date when newspapers appeared, the master advertised his loss, and offered a reward for the return of his apprentice.[18]

As a further check, all persons were strictly forbidden to "harbour or entertain" runaway apprentices. The Code of 1665 is very definite on this point.

> whosoever shall be proved to have Transported, or to have Contrived the Transportation of any such Apprentice or Servant shall forfeit twenty pounds to the Court, and evry Inhabitant that shall harbour or entertain any such Apprentice or Servant, knowing that he had absented himself from his Service, upon due proof thereof shall forfeit to the Master or Dame ten shillings for every Days entertainment or Concealment.[19]

At that date a fine of ten shillings was more or less severe, and it must have operated to reduce the number of such violations. A rather unique newspaper item of 1833 exhibits the practice of this legislation. The article reads:

> A Case in Point — Not long since, a man of the West was prosecuted for employing a Runaway Apprentice, and $100 recovered together with cost of suit which when added to the fee paid his lawyer, and his own personal expenses, amounted, perhaps to the comfortable sum one of hundred and fifty dollars more.
>
> The usual caution was observed by advertising the runaway in the local Newspaper — but the defendant had never taken a Newspaper, and did not know that he was obliged to take one. His wife had subscribed for the New York Observer, and did not believe that the Advertisement was in that. This is as it should be — ignorance, parsimony, and folly should be punished. — Sag Harbor Corrector.[20]

Upon completion of the term of service the apprentice was permitted to follow his trade or calling as a master

---

[18] The Daily Advertiser, New York, Friday, Dec. 19, 1788. "Eight Dollars Reward — Ran away on Thursday night last, from the Ship Pitt, William Dodds master, lying near the New Slip, two Apprentice Boys, one named Geo. Robinson, about 17 or 18 years of age: the other Henry Watt, about 15 years of age."

Diary and Mercantile Advertiser, New York, Wednesday Evening, July 19, 1791. "Five Dollars Reward — Ran away on Thursday, 13th July, an apprentice boy, by the name of George Warner (detailed description follows) . . . Andrew Anderson, cabinet-maker."

[19] Col. Laws of N. Y., I, 36. Repeated Oct. 24, 1684 (*Ibid.*, I, 157).

[20] New York and Richmond County Free Press, Dec. 21, 1833.

"handy Craft" man. The authorities insisted, however, that "he have well and truely Served" his master, or in other words, that he had served a successful apprenticeship. The Duke of York's Laws strictly forbade apprentices "to give sell or truck any Commodity whatsoever dureing the time of theire Service, under penalty of a fine or Corporal punishment, by warrant under the hands of two Justices of the Peace, as the Offence shall meritt."[21] This prohibition operated not only to keep out of the market wares of imperfect quality, which the apprentices might have made, and to protect master craftsmen from the competition of the unskilled, but also to produce skilled workmen, by insisting that the period of apprenticeship be spent in learning their trades. It will be recalled that these restrictions were factors of the early English practice of apprenticeship.[22]

At the same time the apprentice was "made free of the said Citty," i.e., he became a citizen with the right to vote and hold office. No one but "Free Cittyzens" were permitted "to use or exercise Any Art, trade, Mystery or Manual Occupation or . . . sell . . . Any Manner of Merchandize or Wares whatsoever."[23] Since the thirteenth century in England apprenticeship had been a qualification

[21] Repeated Oct. 24, 1684 (Col. Laws of N. Y., I, 157).

[22] Cal. Let. Bk. D, 106, 104, 122, 149, 150, 152, 154, 157. 161, 170, 178.   Cf. New Eng.

[23] Min. Com. Coun. City of N. Y., I, 302.

Ibid., I, 10.   Order of Jan. 20, 1675.

Ibid., I, 103.   This was one of the "seuerall antient Customes . . . granted . . . undr his Royall Highness Anno 1665."

Ibid., I, 137.   "Lawes and Ordors" of Mar. 16, 1683.

Ibid., I, 222, 246; II, 198.   Orders of Apr. 24, 1691; Oct. 15, 1691; July 11, 1702.

Mayors Court Minutes, Nov. 13, 1674 to Apr. 24, 1691.   "Att a Court Meeting held in New Yorke the 5th June in the 27th Yeare of his Matis reigne 1675: The Court having taken into their Consideracon the great inconveniencys of Strangers who come here and openly sell and retayle their goods wares and Merchandize and exercise their trades and handicrafts without taking notice of ye Corporation or obtayning the Privilege of freedom of this Citty according to former Order and Custome as well heere as in other places ordered all such persons to come and address themselves to ye Court and qualify for admission."

of admission into the franchise.[24] As in medieval England there were three methods of obtaining the franchise in the Province of New York: birth, apprenticeship, and redemption. A Common Council of Nov. 9, 1762 ordered that "All and every person or persons hereafter to be made free of this city who were not born within this city, or served a regular apprenticeship of seven years within the same shall pay for the freedom therefore as followeth." [25] But "such as are not able to pay for the same shall be made free Gratis." [26]

Let us turn now to a review of the educational aspects of the legislation just considered. There were only two colonial laws that mentioned the education to be given to apprentices. The first is contained in the Duke of York's Laws of 1665, and the second is a New York City Common Council Order of 1736. Consideration should also be given a State Act of 1788 which repeated part of the requirements of the colonial period, and made it general in application.

The Duke of York's Laws required the instruction of all " Children and Servants in matters of Religion and the Lawes of the Country And that Parents and Masters do bring up their Children and Apprentices in some honest and Lawful Calling Labour and Employment." It will be noted, at this point, that the pauper-apprentices of the Province of New York received not only the "meat drink and lodging," required by the English Poor Law of 1601, but also a certain amount of "learning," and trade training. This aspect of the Code of 1665 will recall the Massachusetts Bay Act of 1642, the New Plymouth Act of 1671, and the Connecticut Code of 1650. Each insisted upon the same requirement —

[24] Chapter I, p. 5.

[25] Appendix to Roll of Freemen, 1695–1774 (N. Y. Hist. Soc. Coll., 1885, 533). Repeated Dec. 2, 1773 (*Ibid.*, 556); Mar. 9, 1784 (Roll of Freemen 1675–1866. N. Y. Hist. Soc. Coll., 1885, 239); Mar. 29, 1786 (*Ibid.*, 274); May 1, 1797 (*Ibid.*, 294); Apr. 27, 1801 (*Ibid.*, 298); Mar. 8, 1815 (*Ibid.*, 399), the last adoption of this law.

[26] Min. Com. Coun. City of N. Y., II, 197. Order of June 27, 1702. Repeated July 11, 1702 (*Ibid.*, II, 199).

" Religion," "Laws," and "some honest and Lawful Calling Labour and Employment." But, in addition, the New England Laws specifically required that all children and apprentices be taught to read. Furthermore they provided the means for the enforcement of this requirement, by ordering that all children whose education had been neglected should be apprenticed to masters "which will more strictly educate and govern them according to the rules of this Order." Apprentices whose education had been neglected were taken away from their masters, and placed with others. While this section of the Duke of York's Laws was a compulsory education law, it did not refer specifically to the apprenticeship system as the means of enforcement. It may be inferred, however, that this use was intended; the framers of the 1665 Code could not have overlooked this important aspect of the New England practice.

Until 1736 the only "learning" required by law for "all Children and Apprentices" in colonial New York, consisted of "Religion and the Lawes of the Country." On March 31 of that year a Common Council of New York City made the following Order:

> That such parish Children as may be hereafter sent to the poorhouse for Maintainance, that Care be taken by the Master there of (by the direction of the Church Wardens and Overseers of the Poor) *that they be religiously educated and taught to read, write, and cast accounts.*[27]

This Order concerned poor-children, but it must not be supposed that they remained very long in the poor-house. That institution was primarily for the maintenance of the adult poor. For the children of poor parents it was a more or less temporary refuge, and they remained there only until the Overseers or Church Wardens could find masters for them. This was never very long; the records of the binding out of poor-children reveal the fact that many were bound out at a very early age. Hence the education received in the poor-house did not go very far into the fields of reading,

---

[27] Min. Com. Coun. City of N. Y., IV, 309.

writing, and casting accounts. But the Order has this significance: it indicates the elementary education requirement of the time for poor-children, at least. And, as we shall see after examining the indentures of apprenticeship, all apprentices received a certain amount of "learning" beyond "Religion and the Lawes of the Country."

On March 7, 1788, the State of New York passed an "Act for the better settlement and relief of the Poor," which contained the following provision for the education of poor-apprentices:

And be it further enacted. . . . That all indentures and contracts to be made by any overseers of the poor of any city or town, by and with the consent of the Justices of the Peace of the County, or any two of them, or by and with the consent of the Mayor, Recorder, and Aldermen, or any two of them, in any city, for binding out any child as an apprentice or servant, shall among the covenants in such indentures or contracts to be made and agreed upon between the parties, always insert a clause to the following effect, "*That every Master and Mistress to whom such child shall be bound as aforesaid, shall cause such child to be taught and instructed to read and write.*" And further That the overseers of the poor for the time being, of each respective city or town shall be guardians of every such child so put and bound out as aforesaid, to take care that the terms of the indentures or contracts and the covenants or agreements therein contained be performed and fulfilled, and that such child be not ill used; and the overseers of the poor are hereby empowered and directed to enquire into the same, and to redress any grievance or grievances in such manner as is prescribed by law.[28]

Prior to this Act there was no general New York legislation that provided for the kind of education to be given to poor-apprentices. But we shall find in actual practice as revealed by the indentures that these requirements were in force from the date of the English occupation, and that they extended to both classes of apprentices.

[28] Laws of N. Y., 11th Session, 1788, 130.

CHAPTER VII

APPRENTICESHIP AND APPRENTICESHIP EDUCATION IN THE PROVINCE OF NEW YORK AS REVEALED BY INDENTURES OF APPRENTICESHIP

THE indenture is the most valuable of apprenticeship records because it sums up the more or less fragmentary account of the practice revealed by legislation and court records. This chapter, which is based on manuscript sources, will present the characteristics of the actual practice, and the educational aspects of the apprenticeship system. For this purpose a great number of indentures will be examined, and the validity of the conclusions will be proportionate to the cumulative effect of the evidence submitted.

The typical indenture of the Province of New York may be represented by the following New York City indenture of May 14, 1705:

This Indenture Witnesseth that Thomas Hill about twelve years of Age with the Consent of William Hollins his father in Law hath put himselfe and by these presents doth voluntarily and of his own free will and accord put himselfe Apprentice unto Christopher Giliard, Cordwainer in the City of New York in America for the space and Term of seaven years Commencing from the date hereof and after the manner of an Apprentice to serve from the Fourteenth day of May one thousand seaven hundred and five untill the full Term of seaven years be Compleat and Ended during all which Term the said Apprentice his said Master and Mistress during the aforesaid Term in the Cordwainer's Trade faithfully shall serve his secrets keep his lawful Commands gladly Every where Obey he shall doe no damage to his said Master nor see to be done by Others without letting or giving Notice thereof to his said Master he shall not waste his said Master's goods nor lend them unlawfully to any, he shall not Commit Fornication nor Contract Matrimony within the said Term att Cards, Dice or any other unlawfull Game he shall not play whereby his said Master may have damage with his own goods nor the goods of others during the said Term without Lycense from his said Master he shall neither buy nor sell he shall not absent himselfe day nor night from his Master's service without his leave nor haunt Ale houses, Taverns or Playhouses but in all things as a faithful Apprentice he shall behave himselfe toward his said Master and all his During the said Term and the said Master during the said Term shall find and provide unto the said Apprentice sufficient meat drinke Apparell Lodging and washing fitting for an Apprentice and after the Expiration of the Said Term of seaven years to give unto his said Apprentice two new suits of Apparell the one for working days the other for Sundays and holy days and to Instruct and teach his said Apprentice in seaven years to read and write English and in the Cordwainer's Trade according to his Ability and for the true performance of all and every the said Covenants and Agreement either of the said parties bind themselves to the other by these presents. In Witness whereof they have interchangeably put their hands and seals this fourteenth day of May in the third Year of the Reign of our sovereign Lady Anne by the Grace of God Queen of England, scotland and France and Ireland etc: Anno Domini one thousand seaven hundred and five Thomas Hill sealed signed and delivered in the presence of us John Sheppard David Vilant New Yorke May ye 14th 1705 Acknowledged by the within named Thomas Hill to be his voluntary Act and Deed. (Signed) William Peartree, Mayor.[1]

This indenture is almost identical in phraseology with some two hundred others examined in this study.

The striking similarity with the earliest English indentures, and with those of New England, will be noted at once. With a few minor changes in phraseology, to conform to the conditions of the particular instance, the same obligations are assumed by each party to the contract. The apprentice bound himself to serve his master "Seaven years," promised to keep his secrets, obey his "Lawful Commands," and "in all things as a faithful Apprentice he shall behave himself." In return the master promised to "find and provide unto the said Apprentice" proper maintenance, teach him his trade, and at the end of the term to give him the customary two suits of "Apparell."[2] In this instance the master also

---

[1] Citty of N. Yorke Indentures of Apprenticeship begun February 19, 1694 and ends Jan. ye 29th 1707, p. 135.

[2] The Duke of York's Laws (1665) required that "All Servants who have served Diligently, and faithfully to the benefit of their Masters and Dames five or Seaven yeares, shall not be Sent empty away." (Col. Laws of N. Y., I, 48) Compare Mass. Body of Liberties of 1641.

promised to teach his apprentice to read and write. As indicated in the treatment of the New England colonies this aspect of the practice of apprenticeship was peculiarly American.

Earlier English legislation, and the laws of the Province of New York insisted upon the registration of all indentures "in the Town Clerkes Office." In compliance with this requirement the indenture before us was enrolled at the City Hall, and signed by the Mayor. All the indentures examined were properly witnessed, and registered with Town Clerks, Aldermen, Justices, or other public officers. The writer found only one case of violation of this requirement.[3]

The terms of the indentures of poor-children were similar to those of voluntary apprentices. But poor-apprentices were bound out by Overseers of the Poor, or Church Wardens, with the "Consent and Approbation" of a "Head Officer." Consequently those officers became parties to the contract, and it was necessary to change the form of the indenture to include their names. The following indenture of this class represents the type:

> This Indenture Witnesses that Isaac Kip & Gerrett Viele Church Wardens and Overseers of the Poor of the Citty of New Yorke by and with the Consent and Approbation of Isaac D: Riemer Esqr Mayor of the said Citty have by these presents placed and bound William Reade a poor fatherless and Motherless Child aged five years unto Robert Nisbett, Taylor . . . untill he the said William Reade Shall Come to the full age of twenty one years According to the Statute in that Case made and Provided . . . (usual form) . . . perfectly to Read and write the English tongue.[4]

The usual term of service in accordance with "the Custome & practice of his Majestys Realm in England, and all the

[3] Page 77.

[4] Citty of N. Yorke Indentures, 68. Dated Sept. 8, 1701.

Ibid., 66. Sept. 8, 1701.

East Hampton Town Records, I, 289. Aug. 26, 1668. This is one of the earliest indentures of poor-children in the Province of New York.

Flushing Town Records, 1790–1833. Manuscript folio volume. See indentures of poor-apprentices, dating from 1806 to 1817, on pages 16, 59, 62, 67, 69, 71, 73, 75, 77, 80, 83, 85, 89, 91, 93, 95, 97, 99, 101, 104, 109, 114.

Adjacent Colonys in America," was seven years. But it will be recalled that a New York City Common Council Act of 1694 permitted four-year terms. Terms as short as three and four years occur occasionally before that date. The majority, however, are for seven years, or until twenty-one. In 1711 a New York City Act required the full seven-year period for all apprentices, and from that time there were but few violations. From 1666 to 1817, 180 out of 220 indentures show compliance with custom in this matter.

Not only were masters required to provide proper maintenance, but the Duke of York's Laws insisted that "Parents and Masters do bring up their Children and apprentices in some honest and Lawful Calling Labour or Employment." The Massachusetts Bay Act of 1642, the New Plymouth Act of 1671, and the Connecticut Code of 1650 contained the same emphasis upon "honest and Lawfull" callings. Useless occupations which would not be "profitable to the Commonwealth," or to the apprentice, were not to be tolerated. Voluntary apprentices received trade training as a matter of routine; they apprenticed themselves for that purpose. If the master defaulted in that regard his apprentice was released from his indenture. Poor-apprentices were not so well taken care of by the Poor Law of 1601, but the colonial laws included them in their general enactments concerning the bringing up of children. In every indenture of the Province and State of New York in which a poor-boy or girl was bound out, trade training was specified among the articles of agreement between master and apprentice.

The indentures show that apprentices were taught such trades as: baker, barber and wig-maker, blacksmith, blockmaker, boatman, brasier, carpenter, cooper, cordwainer, currier, farmer, feltmaker, glasier, glover, goldsmith, gunsmith, hatter, innholder, joiner, leather-dresser, mariner, mason, merchant, painter, pewterer, pipemaker, printer, saddler, sailmaker, seamstress, shipwright, silversmith, skinner, tailor, turner, weaver, wheelwright. Girls were usually taught housewifery, which included "to sew plaine work," and "spinning and knitting"; occasionally they learned the tailor's and glovemaker's trades. The trades enumerated represent fairly well the field of industrial occupation in colonial New York. During the colonial period apprenticeship was also the means of entering the professions of law and medicine. In some instances the schoolmaster may have served an apprenticeship as a preparation for his calling. The following indenture might be of interest at this point:

> Registered for Mr. George Brownell Schoolmaster ye 18th day of July 1722.
>
> This Indenture Witnesseth that John Campbel Son of Robert Campbell of the City of New York with the Consent of his father and mother hath put himself and by these presents doth Voluntarily put and bind himself Apprentice to George Brownell of the Same City Schoolmaster to learn the Art Trade or Mystery . . . for and during the term of ten years. . . . And the said George Brownell Doth hereby Covenant and Promise to teach and Instruct or Cause the said Apprentice to be taught and Instructed in the Art Trade or Calling of a Schoolmaster by the best way or means he or his wife may or can.[5]

In addition to the requirement that all children and apprentices be taught trades, the Code of 1665 demanded that they be given a certain amount of "learning." This, to use the words of the Code, consisted of "Religion and the Lawes of the Country." The New England Acts added reading to this rather limited educational requirement, but the framers of the Duke of York's Laws appear to have overlooked the need of this rudiment. And New York legislation made no reference to a more comprehensive elementary education until 1736, and that was an Act providing for poor-children.[6]

In actual practice we find that the New York apprentice received an education equal to that which the New England apprentice enjoyed. One of the earliest indentures of the Province of New York, dated April 16, 1666, contains the covenant of the master to teach his apprentice "reading and wrighting."[7] This provision remained the most popular throughout the colonial

---

[5] Citty of N. Yorke Indentures, 145–47.   [6] Page 86.
[7] Newtown Town Records, 1663–1695, 159.   Manuscript.

period.[8]   In some instances the apprentice was taught only to read,[9] or write,[10] or cypher;[11] in others he received reading and cyphering,[12] or writing and cyphering.[13]   The most complete education given to apprentices consisted of reading, writing, and cyphering.[14]   Girls received instruction in reading,[15] or reading and writing.[16]   The records do not reveal a single instance in which a girl was taught to cypher, or "cast accounts."

The question now arises: where was the apprentice taught to "read and writt," or to "Read right and Syfer"?   Accord-

[8] The following indentures of 1683–1729 provide for reading and writing: Records of the Town of Easthampton, II, 131, 133; Westchester Town Records, 1664–1696 (Manuscript), 160, 161, 165, 167, 249; Westchester Records, 1707–1720 (Manuscript), 252, 262; Citty of N. Yorke Indentures, 12, 39, 52, 61, 66, 68, 110, 112, 113, 119, 135, 145, 147; Liber 29, 5, 44, 55, 59, 69, 73, 83, 117, 119, 164, 178, 192, 206, 212, 234, 296, 329, 353; First Book of the Supervisors of Dutchess County, 19; Records of North and South Hempstead, III, 51; Mayors Court Minutes, Jan. 26, 1724 to June 1729, action dated Dec. 24, 1729.   This provision continues in the early state period.   See the following indentures of 1806–1817, in Flushing Town Records, 1790–1833 (Manuscript), 16, 59, 62, 65, 67, 69, 71, 73, 75, 77, 80, 83, 86, 89, 91, 93, 95, 97, 99, 101, 104, 109, 114.

[9] Harlem Records, II, 543 (Manuscript).   Indenture of Oct. 14, 1700.   See indenture of Feb. 18, 1763, in Huntington Town Records, II, 454.

[10] Citty of N. Yorke Indentures, 54.   Indenture of Aug. 12, 1700.

[11] Flushing Town Records, 1790–1833.   Indenture of Jan. 4, 1817.

[12] Newtown Records, 1714–1753, 24.   Indenture of July 12, 1713.

[13] See the following indentures of 1701–1723: Citty of N. Yorke Indentures, 82, 94, 100; Liber 29, 32, 34, 36, 97, 102, 142, 147, 152, 154, 193.

[14] See the following indentures of 1700–1740: Citty of N. Yorke Indentures, 46, 98, 105, 144, 157; Liber 29, 4, 76, 80, 170, 176, 190, 197, 216, 225, 229, 241, 256, 266, 276, 278, 280, 282, 305, 311, 314, 321, 324, 354; Westchester Records, 1707–1720, 254½; Westchester Records, 1711–1730 (Manuscript. Pages not numbered); Newtown Records, 1714–1753, 101; Huntington Town Records, II, 494, 518; Records of North and South Hempstead, III, 241; Mayors Court Minutes, May 1722 to May 1742, action dated May 6, 1735.   See also indentures of 1816 and 1817, in Flushing Town Records, 1790–1833, 104, 109.

[15] See the following indentures of 1680–1726: Huntington Town Records, I, 275; Citty of N. Yorke Indentures, 22, 31, 58, 86, 97; Newtown Records, 1700–1714 (Manuscript), 178; Westchester Records, 1707–1720, 242¾, 253 (Manuscript); Jamaica Town Records, III, 1706–1749, 299; Liber 29, 75, 174, 204, 218, 263, 292, 341.

[16] See the following indentures of 1683–1725: Records of the Town of Easthampton, II, 131; Liber 29, 64, 72, 137, 273, 329.   See also indentures of 1806–1817, in Flushing Town Records, 1790–1833: 59, 65, 75, 80, 86, 89, 91, 93, 97, 99, 101, 114.

ing to the indenture the master promised to "teach or cause him to be taught." But many masters were illiterate. This fact is borne out by the indentures of apprenticeship, a large number of which were signed with the masters' marks in lieu of signatures. In such cases masters did not teach their apprentices, but "caused" them "to be taught." This meant that many apprentices were sent to school.

Ono of the earliest references to the practice of sending apprentices to school occurs in a Harlem indenture dated Nov. 25, 1690, in which the master promised that his apprentice "shall have the privelege of going to the evening school."[17] According to a New York City indenture of Oct. 1, 1698, the apprentice was to be given "his winter's schooling."[18] From indentures of a later date we learn that the evening school was kept in the winter. An indenture of Nov. 18, 1701, contains the provision: "in the Evenings to go to School Each Winter to the End he may be taught to write and read."[19] In some instances the master promised to give his apprentice "One Quarter of a year's Schooling,"[20] in others "Every winter three Months Evening Schooling."[21] An indenture dated Jan. 20, 1720, combines the two preceding provisions into "a Quarter or three Months Schooling in every Winter."[22] And the particular three months, or quarter, during which the evening school was held is indicated in an indenture of Feb. 24, 1719, in which the master agreed to "put him to school three Months in Every Year during the said apprenticeship Immediately after Christmas in Every Year to the Evening School to learn to Read and

[17] Harlem Records, II, 529 (Manuscript).

[18] Citty of N. Yorke Indentures, 47. See also Harlem Records, II, 543; Citty of N. Yorke Indentures, 90, 81, 155; Liber 29, 19, 7, 31, 60, 67, 73, 117, 230, for indentures of 1698–1724.

[19] *Ibid.*, 81.

[20] *Ibid.*, 60, Indenture of Jan. 20, 1700. See also indentures of 1718–1726 in: Liber 29, 1, 39, 54, 14, 83, 110, 123, 129, 152, 156, 181, 196, 199, 220, 227, 241, 244, 261, 264, 266, 268, 270, 275, 284, 286, 303, 312, 314, 324, 325, 327, 354, 358.

[21] *Ibid.*, 62, 107, 128, 143, 158; Liber 29, 3, 13, 44, 45, 55, 59, 70, 86, 90, 102, 112, 119, 151, 158, 168, 172, 216, 232, 239, 242, 320, 349. Indentures of 1701–1726.

[22] Liber 29, 94.

Write." [23] Frequently the indentures refer to these three months as "the usual times in the Winter Evenings," or the "Customary" period.[24] That the evening school was held only at this time is indicated by these references, and by an indenture of June 9, 1726, in which the apprentice is "to go to School during the time that is customary here to keep Night School." [25]

The records also reveal the fact that there was more than one evening school in New York City. An indenture of Oct. 17, 1705, contains the master's covenant "to lett him (the apprentice) have in Every Winter three Months Learning *att any Evening School within this City*, and to pay for the same." [26] Another master, in 1720, agreed to send his apprentice "One Quarter of a Year in Each Year of the said Term to a good Evening School." [27] A 1690 indenture mentioned above reveals the existence of an evening school in Harlem, which was within the jurisdiction of New York City.

It may be fairly assumed that many New York apprentices went to evening schools. As a rule apprentices could not be spared during the day; they were more or less constantly employed by their masters. Thrifty schoolmasters keen to take advantage of this situation opened evening schools. The writer found one hundred and eight indentures which contained provisions for sending apprentices to evening schools. Of this number not one indicates that girls attended these schools. It is safe to say that they did not. Some few girl-apprentices did attend day-schools, however.

---

[23] *Ibid.*, 55. See also *Ibid.*, 123, indenture of July 30, 1705: "to allow him Evening Schooling Every Winter from Christmas as is Customary"; 139, indenture of Jan. 18, 1722: "Schooling in Winter Evenings from Christmas"; 289, indenture of June 1, 1725: "Every Quarter after Christmas"; 346, indenture of May 1, 1726: "Eavening scholling from Christemis Eavery year of the said term."

[24] *Ibid.*, 34, 36, 102, 212, 216, 225. Indentures of 1717–1724.

[25] *Ibid.*, 318.

[26] Citty of N. Yorke Indentures, 128.

[27] Liber 29, 80.

An indenture of June 11, 1724, contains the following provision for a girl: "Schooling to Learn to read." [28]   A certain number of apprentices, boys and girls, attended schools conducted by the Society for the Propagation of the Gospel in Foreign Parts, and it is probable that the education of many poor-apprentices was taken care of by this society.

The province of New York made no provision for establishing free evening schools.   These schools were privately conducted, and tuition-fees were charged.   It was customary for the master to pay all charges for the instruction of his apprentices.   Sometimes this was specifically mentioned in the indenture: the master "shall at his own Charge put his said Apprentice to School." [29]   In one instance the apprentice was "to go to the winter Evening School at the Charge of his father"; [30]   and in another, it was agreed that the apprentice should go to "Night School three Months in every Year dureing the said term his father to pay one halfe of Said Schooling and his Master the other halfe." [31]   But these were exceptions;   the master in most cases assumed all expenses of maintaining and educating his apprentices.

The curriculum of the evening schools conformed to the educational needs of the New York apprentice.   According to the records they offered instruction in reading, writing, and cyphering.   The evidence of the indentures indicates that these subjects were taught singly, or in any combination desired.   An indenture of Oct. 14, 1700, provides for sending

[28] Liber 29, 218.

[29] *Ibid.*, 36.   Indenture of Aug. 1, 1717.

Ibid., 128.   Indenture of Oct. 17, 1705: master "to pay for the same"; 14. Indenture of Dec. 4, 1717; 5.   Indenture of Sept. 1, 1718: "at the Charge of the said Master"; 15.   Indenture of Oct. 15, 1718; 90.   Indenture of May 1, 1719; 32.   Indenture of Aug. 1, 1719: "Masters Cost and Charge"; 158.   Indenture of Feb. 7, 1722; 236.   Indenture of Feb. 26, 1723: "at my one Cost and Charge"; 327.   Indenture of Nov. 26, 1725.

[30] *Ibid.*, 31.

[31] *Ibid.*, 13.

Citty of N. Yorke Indentures, 90.   Indenture of Oct. 20, 1701: "the father shall provide and pay for two winters Nights scooling and his said Master Shall allow him two halfe Winters Schooling."

the apprentice to the "winter school *to learn to read* as long as the school time shall last." [32] In other instances the apprentice was permitted "in the evenings to go to School Each Winter to the End that he may be taught *to write and Read*," [33] or to "Learn *Writing and Cyphering* at the usuall Winter Seasons." [34] The most popular provision, however, was: "One Quarter of a Year in Each Year of said Term to a good Evening School in Order to be well instructed in *reading writing Accounting* and the like." [35]

It is interesting to note the content of the course in "cyphering," or arithmetic, pursued by the apprentice. A

[32] Harlem Records, II, 543.
[33] Citty of N. Yorke Indentures, 81. Indenture of Nov. 18, 1701.
See the following indentures, in Liber 29:
59 (Feb. 9, 1719): "three Months to School to Learn to Write and Read."
55 (Feb. 24, 1719): "School . . . Every Year . . . to learn to Read and Write."
69 (Dec. 9, 1719): "school at Suitable Times . . . to learn to Read and Write."
83 (Apr. 26, 1720): "Schooling to Read and Write."
119 (Nov. 18, 1720): "Every Winter . . . Evening School . . . to Read and Write."
127 (Nov. 24, 1720): "Read and write . . . in Evening School."
117 (Feb. 1, 1721): "Evening Schooling . . . to Read and write English."
212 (July 10, 1722): "to Read and write English . . . in Winter Evenings."
[34] Liber 29, 36. Indenture of Aug. 1, 1717. See the following in Liber 29:
36 (Aug. 1, 1717): "School to Learn Writing and Cyphering."
78 (Apr. 16, 1718): "Evening School . . . to learn to write and cypher."
34 (Aug. 6, 1719): "to write and cypher at the usual times in the winter."
102 (May 1, 1720): "School . . . Evenings to Learn Writing and Cyphering."
193 (Sept. 1, 1723): "Night School . . . writeing and Arithmetick."
[35] Liber 29, 80. Indenture of Aug. 1, 1720. See the following in Liber 29:
82 (Nov. 8, 1720): "Evening School . . . Reading and Writing and Arithmetick."
190 (Nov. 6, 1722): "Schooling to Read write and Arithmetick."
241 (Jan. 31, 1723): "Evening School to Read write and Cypher."
197 (Aug. 1, 1723): "School . . . on Winter Evenings . . . to Read write and Cypher."
266 (Dec. 25, 1723): "Every Winter one Quarter . . . to Read writ and Cypher."
314 (Jan. 4, 1724): "Every Winter . . . Evenen Skool . . . to Read write en syfer."
225 (July 26, 1724): "School . . . in the Winter . . . to Reade write and Cypher."
278 (Oct. 5, 1724): "Winters to School . . . to Read write and Cypher."
229 (Oct. 26, 1724): "Winter Season . . . to School . . . to Reade write Cypher."
280 (June 1, 1725): "Reading writing and Cyphering at the Cost . . . of Master."
289 (June 1, 1725): "to read and write . . . every Quarter . . . and Syfer two Quarters."

Westchester indenture of July 1, 1716, makes provision for teaching the apprentice to "Read Write & Cast Accompts to so far as the Rule of three." [36] Sometimes this description was added to in the following manner: "Cypher as far as the rule of three direct inclusive." [37] The most complete statement of the composition of this subject occurs in a New York City indenture of May 20, 1720, in which the master agreed to provide instruction in "writing and cyphering So far as Addition Subtraction and Multiplication." [38] In some instances the apprentice was to be taught "to Cypher so as to keep his Own accounts," [39] or "so far as he be able to keep his Booke." [40]

[36] Westchester Records, 1707–1720, 254½.

[37] Flushing Town Records, 1790–1833, 104. Indenture of Oct. 31, 1816.

Ibid., 16. Indenture of Jan. 4, 1817: "to cypher as far as the rule of three direct."

[38] Liber 29, 97.

[39] *Ibid.*, 276. Indenture of Feb. 1, 1722.

[40] Westchester Records, 1711–1730 (Pages not numbered). July 23, 1725.

Huntington Town Records, II, 518. Indenture of Sept. 7, 1772: "to read write & Arethmatick so as to keep a good Book."

CHAPTER VIII

APPRENTICESHIP AND THE EDUCATION OF APPRENTICES IN THE PROVINCE OF NEW YORK, AS REVEALED BY WILLS

ANOTHER source of information concerning apprenticeship, and the education of apprentices in the Province of New York is the collection of New York wills dating from 1665 to 1786.[1] One of the earliest wills, dated March 16, 1669, reads as follows:

> Abraham Jossling, Nashua . . . "Being very sick" . . . Leaves to wife one House in Nashaway, with land thereto belonging . . . . To eldest son Abraham "One farm that Goodman Kittle lives on.". . ."And Good wife I would not have you remane where you are with any of my children, but *my desire is that my children may be put out to Trades.*"[2]

Some wills direct that "My two sons . . . shall be bound out to learn *some suitable trade*,"[3] or "*some good trade.*"[4] Occasionally the executors were instructed to select the trade; in one instance "My two sons are to be put to learn trades *at the discretion of my executors*,"[5] in another, "My son John . . . is to be put to learn a trade *which my executors think proper.*"[6] In a few cases the trade was specified in the will,

---

[1] Abstracts of Wills, 1665–1786, N. Y. Hist. Soc. Coll., 1892–1908. 17 vols.

[2] *Ibid.*, I, 14.

Ibid., V, 198 (Dec. 6, 1750); 29 (May 18, 1754); 103 (Apr. 22, 1756); 179 (Feb. 16, 1757); 192 (July 3, 1757); 321 (June 7, 1759); 359 (Dec. 30, 1759); VI, 53 (Feb. 19, 1761); 126 (Nov. 2, 1761); 142 (Jan. 25, 1762); 230 (Dec. 16, 1762); 248 (Mar. 19, 1763).

[3] *Ibid.*, III, 296 (Moriches, May 5, 1736).

Ibid., II, 236 (East Hampton, Feb. 6, 1712).

[4] *Ibid.*, IV, 106 (Oyster Bay, Nov. 9, 1746).

Ibid., VI, 108 (Sept. 29, 1761); 158 (Dec. 8, 1761).

[5] *Ibid.*, II, 365 (Southampton, Sept. 14, 1725).

[6] *Ibid.*, IV, 384 (Hempstead, Apr. 22, 1746).

Ibid., I, 257 (N. Y. City, Apr. 29, 1695): "putting them to such trades as they be thought most capable to learn"; I, 342 (N. Y. City, Aug. 3, 1702): "they

as: "desiring that as soon as it is convenient she may learn the trade of a Tayler," [7] and "bring up my son William to good Common Learning, and at a fit time bind him out as an apprentice to a Smith." [8] The most common practice, however, was to leave instructions for putting a boy "to learn a trade as he best Likes, and likewise schooling," [9] or "a trade that he shall reasonably choose." [10]

The children mentioned in these wills were bound out at a later age than the apprentices considered in the preceding chapter. This may account for the fact that many of them were permitted to learn the trades of their own selection. A brief inventory of the estates justifies the statement that the parents of these children were relatively well-to-do. Hence they could provide, as they did, for a longer period of maintenance, and bringing-up at home. A Southampton will dated Jan. 3, 1711, instructs the executors "to provide for Uriah . . . till he is fourteen years of age and then he is to be put to a trade." [11] In other instances the

are to be instructed in reading and writing, and an art or trade each according to their ability." It is probable that the executor in each of these cases exercised his discretion as to the "capacity" of the children to learn certain trades.

Abstracts of Wills, VI, 220 (Dec. 25, 1762).

[7] *Ibid.*, I, 375 (Hempstead, Apr. 2, 1702).

[8] *Ibid.*, III, 286 (Goshen, Feb. 9, 1739).

[9] *Ibid.*, III, 2 (Kingston, May 9, 1730).

Ibid., II, 362 (N. Y. City, July 10, 1716): "bring up the children in the fear of God, and allow them instruction in an art or trade or mysterie according to the sex and inclination of every child."

[10] *Ibid.*, IV, 384 (Huntington, Mar. 27, 1750).

Ibid., VI, 426 (Southold, May 30, 1765): "My sons Warren and Daniel are to be bound out to learn a trade which they may choose, when they are 14 years old."

[11] *Ibid.*, II, 138.

Ibid., II, 192 (Southampton, Dec. 15, 1718): "To support the children till the youngest is fourteen years of age, and be bound out to learn some trade."

Ibid., V, 115 (N. Y. City): "till he is 14 years of age and then bound apprentice to some good trade."

Ibid., V, 167 (Hempstead, Mar. 6, 1757): "till they are 14 years old and then put to trades."

Ibid., V, 175 (Goshen, Apr. 17, 1757): "My son James is to be put out to a trade when he is 14."

boy "is to be put to learn a trade when he is 15,"[12] or sixteen years of age.[13]   Sometimes the children "are to be put to trades when of suitable age,"[14] or "when they are fit for the same."[15]   The customary age at which children of this class were apprenticed seems to have been about fourteen.

"Until such time as they are fit to be put to trades,"[16] the children of parents who left adequate estate were to "be brought up in general with schooling sufficient for them."[17]   The typical provision for this preliminary education is contained in a Flushing will dated Nov. 30, 1759, which directed that "My children are to be put at school

Ibid., V, 384 (Westchester, Mar. 24, 1760): "My executors are to sell all the rest of my movable estate, all debts to be paid, and the remainder used to maintain my other children, viz., Thomas, James, Frederick, and Augustine, until they are 14, at which age they are to be bound out to trades until of age. . . . My reputed daughter Elizabeth . . . they are to maintain her till she is 14 years old, and then bind her till she is of age."

Ibid., VI, 241 (East Chester, Apr. 7, 1763): "My sons are to be put to trades at the age of fourteen."

Ibid., VI, 426 (Southold, May 30, 1765): "when they are 14 years old."

[12] *Ibid.*, II, 312 (Brookhaven, June 30, 1718).

Ibid., 124 (Brookhaven, Mar. 23, 1746): "my son is to be put out to learn a trade when he is 15 years of age."

Ibid., IV, 384 (Huntington, Mar. 27, 1750):   "My son Edmond, when he is 15 years of age, is to be put to a trade."

[13] *Ibid.*, VI, 289 (Hempstead, June 8, 1763): "And they shall allow to my grandson John Charlock, sufficient meat, drink, lodging, and apparell until he is 16, and then put him to a good trade."

[14] *Ibid.*, IV, 443 (Flushing, Mar. 29, 1752).

Ibid., VI, 19 (Richmond County, Nov. 2, 1760): "when of suitable age."

Ibid., IV, 419 (N. Y. City, Aug. 27, 1752): "at a proper season to put them to learn a trade."

Ibid., VI, 130 (Fordham, May 6, 1761).

Ibid., VI, 311 (Flushing, Jan. 15, 1764): "My sons John and Thomas are to be put to good trades when of sufficient age."

[15] *Ibid.*, III, 48 (Brookland, Jan. 18, 1731).

Ibid., III, 286 (Goshen, Feb. 9, 1739): "at a fit time to bind him out as an apprentice to a Smith."

Ibid., IV, 334 (North Castle, Westchester Co., Feb. 25, 1751).

Ibid., VI, 394 (N. Y. City, Jan. 26, 1765): "to be put out when they are fit."

[16] *Ibid.*, IV, 334 (Westchester, Feb. 25, 1751).

[17] *Ibid.*, IV, 369 (Oyster Bay, June 28, 1751).

till such times as they are fit to put to trades."[18] Sometimes the duration of the "schooling" was fixed, as in the
following will: "My two younger sons, Gilbert and Jacob,
are to be kept at school till they are 14 years old and then
put to trades."[19] The provisions were usually very definite
in specifying the kind of education to be obtained at school,
as: "reading and writing,"[20] or "wreading, writing and arith-
mitick."[21] In one instance the executors were instructed
"to larn him to write and sifer so as to keep a common
tradesmans book,"[22] in another, the boy was to be taught
"reading and in Arithmatick so far as is needful to keep a
book of Accounts."[23] It may not be inappropriate at this

[18] Abstracts of Wills, V, 363.

Ibid., III, 2 (Kingston, May 9, 1730).

Ibid., III, 212 (Albany, July, 20, 1736).

Ibid., IV, 198 (Hunting Grove, Ulster Co., May 29, 1742).

Ibid., IV, 76 (Hempstead, Apr. 22, 1746): "My son John is to go to school till
he has Good Learning and then to be put to learn a trade."

Ibid., IV, 193 (Newburgh, Feb. 25, 1747): "Schooling my children till they are
fit to put to trades."

Ibid., V, 147 (Oyster Bay, Feb. 16, 1755).

Ibid., VI, 19 (Richmond County, Nov. 2, 1760).

Ibid., VI, 251 (Hempstead, Feb. 11, 1763).

[19] *Ibid.*, V, 167 (Hempstead, Mar. 6, 1557).

[20] *Ibid.*, I, 342 (N. Y. City, Aug. 3, 1702).

Ibid., I, 143 (N. Y. City, Mar. 12, 1676): "the children are to be caused to learn
to read and write, and a trade."

Ibid., I, 121 (N. Y. City, June 16, 1680). Girl: "reading and writing, and a
trade."

Ibid., II, 441 (N. Y. City, Feb. 23, 1685): "to read and write, and a trade."

Ibid., I, 236 (N. Y. City, July 24, 1686): "to read and write, and an art or trade."

Ibid., I, 209 (N. Y. City, May 15, 1691): "to read and write, and afterwards a
trade."

Ibid., I, 257 (N. Y. City, Apr. 29, 1695): "to read and write, and putting them
to trades."

Ibid., II, 67 (Albany, June 26, 1710): "to read and write and some lawful
trade."

[21] *Ibid.*, VI, 51 (Rochester, Feb. 9, 1759).

Ibid., I, 133 (Albany, Aug. 6, 1683): "reading, writing, and Arithmetic, and
. . . trade."

Ibid., V, 320 (Dec. 18, 1757): "at School to larn to read, write, and Syfer."

[22] *Ibid.*, VI, 262 (Southold, July 11, 1763).

[23] *Ibid.*, V, 328 (Brookhaven, May 4, 1759).

point to quote from another will which throws additional light on the content of arithmetic, or "cyphering," in the colonial period. The will of John Little of Stonefield, Ulster County, dated May 13, 1752, provides as follows:

> My executors are to keep my grand son, John McGarrach, at school till he learns to read and write English and *the five common rules of Arithmatick* and then bind him to a house carpenter or any other good trade.[24]

In some cases wealthier parents provided for a more extended education as a preliminary to learning a trade, such as is indicated in the following will:

> My friend George Home is to be the guardian of my said son, and at the age of five years he is to be sent to Great Britain, with a sufficiency to put him to some good school or Academy to be taught English and Latin and accounts till he is fourteen years of age and then bound apprentice to some good trade.[25]

Very probably it was a more or less common practice for the wealthy to send their children to academies in England.

[24] *Ibid.*, V, 273.   [25] *Ibid.*, V, 115 (N.Y. City, Apr. 26, 1755).

CHAPTER IX

CONCLUSION

THE evidence submitted in the preceding chapters indicates that the essential characteristics of the English practice of apprenticeship were reproduced in colonial New England and New York. In the mother-country the practice dated from the late thirteenth, and early fourteenth centuries; it appeared in the colonies with the earliest settlers. As soon as the colonists took under consideration the business of making laws for their new settlements, they turned their attention to the apprenticeship system. English custom and law obtained to regulate the practice, but the colonists saw in it new and broader possibilities of use.

The problem of providing an elementary education for all children, and trade training for those not of independent estate was important and pressing; the law of 1642 states that there had been "great neglect in many parents and masters in training up their children in labor and learning." But the solution was not far to seek. The inhabitants of Massachusetts Bay saw in the apprenticeship system, already established, an effective instrument for compelling the education of all youth. In order to accomplish this purpose, however, it was necessary to enact new legislation. The Massachusetts Bay colonists had originated a brand-new idea; there was nothing in English law or custom that could serve as a determining precedent for this scheme. The outcome of their deliberation was the famous General Court Order of 1642, which laid upon all parents and masters the obligation to teach their children and apprentices "to read and understand the principles of religion and the capital laws of the country," and to give them training in employments which would be profitable to themselves and "to the Commonwealth." To enforce this requirement the Selectmen were instructed to visit regularly all parents and masters within their districts, and ascertain whether the children were being educated in the prescribed requirements. Where they discovered cases of neglect, the Selectmen were ordered to take children from their parents, and apprentices from their masters, and bind them out to persons who would observe the law. To insure the prompt and efficient performance of their duty, the law provided that the Selectmen "shall be liable to be punished and fined for the neglect thereof."

An elementary education limited to the requirements of the Act of 1642 could not long satisfy the needs of the growing colony, and soon there appeared a fairly widespread demand for a more practical course. The records indicate that, in the absence of new legislation on the subject, masters were meeting this demand themselves, by giving their apprentices instruction in reading, writing, and arithmetic. And it was not until 1703 that the colony recognised this need. In that year a Poor-Law was enacted which required that poor-apprentices be taught to read and write. Successive Poor-Laws enacted in the years 1710, 1720, 1731, 1741, and 1771 indicate the development of the elementary educational requirement until it was given its most comprehensive statement — "males, reading, writing, and cyphering; females, reading and writing." While these laws were primarily intended to provide for the education of poor children, they applied to all children just as the Act of 1642 did (See Act of July 3, 1735).

As we have seen, from our examination of the records, the law was generally well observed. In the few instances where elementary education was neglected, the apprenticeship system operated automatically to remedy the delinquency. This apprenticeship Act constitutes the first compulsory education law in America, and it is worthy of note that it was not until two centuries later that the State of Massachusetts passed its first compulsory education law.

The example of Massachusetts Bay was quickly followed by each of the remaining New England colonies. The Connecticut Code of 1650, the New Haven Code of 1655, and the New Plymouth General Court Order of 1671 reproduced almost verbatim the significant requirements of the Act of 1642. And the practice, as revealed by town records and indentures of apprenticeship, indicates that the new system operated fairly successfully. The colony of Rhode Island and Providence Plantations enacted no legislation comparable to these Acts, but the practice of apprenticeship was adopted without colony or town action, and served the same purposes.

The first provision made for education in the Province of New York was the extension of the educational requirements of the apprenticeship system. This was contained in the Duke of York's Laws of 1665, which "strictly required" the instruction of all children and apprentices "in matters of Religion and the Lawes of the Country . . . and in some honest and Lawful Calling." From the tenor of this law, and from the fact that the entire Code of 1665 had been "collected out of the several laws now in force in his Majesty's American colonies and plantations," it is evident that its essential features were borrowed from the New England laws. Each Act emphasized the principle that all children must be brought up in learning and labor. In addition, the New England laws specifically required that all children and apprentices be taught to read. The New York law was clearly a compulsory education law, but, unlike the New England codes, it did not refer to the apprenticeship system as the means of enforcement. That this was intended, however, is borne out by the practice as revealed by indentures and other records.

In the colonies considered apprentices were sent to schools where masters were incapable of giving the required instruction. The masters paid the tuition-charges, and, in Massachusetts, those who could not afford to pay the necessary fees were aided by the town. In the New England colonies these schools were day-schools, while in New York the records refer only to evening-schools. It is probable that the evening-schools were opened especially for apprentices, who were not free to attend in the day-time. These schools were not free, and the tuition-fees were paid by the masters. The indentures of apprenticeship reveal the fact that there was an evening school in the Royal Colony of New York as early as 1690, and that by 1705 several had been opened. Like the New England day-schools the evening-schools of New York offered instruction in reading, writing, and arithmetic — the customary elementary curriculum.

It is interesting to note that the legislative provisions for the kind of education to be given to apprentices, in both the New England and New York colonies, is contained in Poor-Laws. The indentures and other records indicate that they applied to voluntary industrial-apprentices as well as to poor-apprentices. There was no separate legislation concerning the education of the former class.

In New England and New York the first laws concerning education, and the first compulsory education laws were contained in apprenticeship enactments. As we have seen, the apprenticeship system took care of the entire problem of public elementary education during the colonial period. By the enactment of these laws the scope of apprenticeship was broadened to such an extent that it became a new, and peculiarly American institution.

APPENDIX A

TRANSCRIPT OF AN INDENTURE PRESERVED AT NORWICH,
DATED JUNE 10, 1291

*From Hudson and Tingey, The Records of the City of Norwich,
Vol. I, 245*

Mem. quod hec est conuencio facta inter Johannem filium Gerardi le
Specer de Norwyco ex parte una et Hubertum filium Willelmi di Tiben-
ham de Gernemutha ex parte altera videlicet quod predictus Hubertus
stabit in seruicio predicti Johannis continue a festo Pentecoste anno
regni regis Edwardi filii Henrici regis decimo nono usque ad terminum
sex annorum proxime subsequentium plenarie completorum, eidem
Johanni in omnibus prout decet humilite fideliter competenter pro
posse suo interim deseruiendo. Et predictus Hubertus erit apprenticius dicti Johannis per totum dictum tempus. Et precepta eius diligenter faciet per totum et secreta sua que fuerint concelanda firmiter
concelabit et a seruicio dicti Johannis in terminum nullo modo recedet
nisi ab ipso Johanne prius jure et racione fuerit licenciatus. Et non
licebit dicto Johanni infra dictum terminum dictum Hubertum amouere
de seruicio suo nisi ex racionabili et probabili causa. Et predictus Hubertus per totum dictum tempus fideliter et honorifice custodiet et ap-
probabit bona et catalla Johannis in cunctis locis quando ipsi Huberto
fuerint commendata et inde fideliter dicto Johanni respondebit. Et
illa bona nullis dabit nec accomodabit sim licencia et speciali mandatu
domini sui. Et predictus Hubertus infra dictum tempus nullo modo
dampnum dicto Johanni faciet et maliciose ad valenciam vj denariorum
vel amplius neque dampnum aut pudorem dicto Johanni in terminum in
aliquo videbit imminere quin allud impediat pro posse suo vel ipsum
Johannem inde premuniat nec aliquam contencionem infra dictum terminum facere aut mouere inter vicinos et mercatores ex quo dictus Johannes aliquo modo poterit agrauari. Et si dictus Hubertus in aliquo
contra premisse euenerit ipse Hubertus et eius fideiussores subscripti
secundum consideracionem mercatorem et aliorem virorum fide dig-
norum inde dicto Johanni respondebunt et satisfacient competenter.
Et si dictus Johannes decesserit infra dictum tempus dictus Hubertus
seruiet assignato idoneo dicto Johanni cuicunque ipsum legauerit qui
sit eiusdem officii usque in finem dicti termini plenarie in omnibus

sicuti dicto Johanni fecerit si superstes fuisset. Et dictus Johannes per totum tempus docebit dictum Hubertum officium suum quo utitur emendi vendendi et omnia alia faciendi que ad illud officium suum pertinent diligenter competente pro posse suo secundum ipsius Huberti ingenii capacitatem. Et idem Johannes vel eius assignatus per totum dictum tempus inueniet dicto Huberto cibos et potum vestimenta linea et calciamenta et unam supertunicam vel tunicam singulis annis infra iij ultimos annos dicti termini prout decet talem erudientum habere. Et si predictus Hubertus quocunque anno dicti termini moriatur vel si predictus Hubertus cum dicto Johanne nullo modo stare poterit propter duritiam vel asperitatem ipsius Johannis vel eius assignati tunc dictus Johannes vel eius assignatus restituet dicto Huberto vel eius fideiussoribus quolibet anno qui retro fuerit dicti termini dimidiam maream argenti. Pro qua quidem erudicione et pro predicta sustentacione dicto Huberto per predictum tempus inuenienda dictus Hubertus dedit dicto Johanni xl solidos sterlingorum pre manibus ad omnia premissa ex ultraque parte obseruanda. Predictus Johannes et Hubertus inuenerunt alternatim fideiussores. (Fideiussores) dicti Huberti sunt Adam de Sahem, Rogerus de Morle. Et fideiussores dicti Johannis sunt Willelmus frater eius, Radulphus Boleman. In cuius rei testimonium huic scripto in modo Cyrographi, confecto sigilla partium et fideiussorum alternatim sunt appensa. Testibus Willelmo de Scothowe, Willelmo de Kyrkeby, Gilberto de Erlham, Rogero de Apeton et aliis.''

INDENTURE OF APPRENTICESHIP, 1396

From the Archaeological Journal, London, 1872, Vol. XXIX, 184.

Haec Indentura testatur quod ita convenit inter Johannem Hyndlee de Norhampton, Brasyer, ex parte une, et Thomam Edward, filium Gilberti Edward de Wyndesore, ex parte altera, quod praedictus Thomas Edward semetipsum fecit et posuit apprenticium dicto Johanni Hyndlee, ad deserviendum eidem Johanni Hyndlee et assignatis suis bene et fideliter more apprenticii a festo omnium sanctorum proxime futuro post datam presentium usque ad finem septem annorum proxime extunc sequentium et plenarie completorum, ad artem vocatam brasyer's craft, qua dictus Johannes utitur, medio tempore humiliter erudiendum. Infra quem quidem terminum dictorum septem annorum praefatus Thomas Edward consilia dicti Johannis Hyndlee magistri sui celanda celabit. Dampnum eidem Johanni magistro suo nullo modo faciet nec fieri videbit, quin illud cito impediet aut dictum magistrum suum statim inde premuniet. A servicio suo praedicto seipsum illicito non absentabit. Bona et catalla dicti Johannis magistri sui absque ejus licencia nulli accomodabit. Tabernam, scortum, talos, aleas, et joca similia non frequentabit, in dispendium magistri sui praedicti. Fornicationem nec adulterium cum aliqua muliere de domo et familia dicti Johannis magistri sui nullo modo committet, neque uxorem ducet, absque licencia magistri sui praedicti. Praecepta et mandata licita et racionabilia dicti Johannis magistri sui ubique pro fideli posse ipsius Thomae, diligenter adimplebit et eisdem mandatis libenter obediet, durante toto termino suo praenotato. Et, si praedictus Thomas de aliqua convencione sua vel articulo praescrito defecerit, tunc idem Thomas juxta modum et quantitatem delicti sui praefato Johanni magistro suo satisfaciet emendam aut terminum apprenticiatus sui praedicti duplicabit, iterando servicium suum praefixum. Et praefatus Johannes Hyndlee at assignati sui dictum Thomam apprenticium suum in arte praedicta melioro modo quo idem Johannes sciverit ac poterit tractabunt, docebunt et informabunt, seu ipsum informari facient sufficienter, debito modo castigando, et non aliter. Praeterea dictus Johannes concedit ad docendum et informandum dictum Thomam in arte vocata Peuterer's craft adeo bene sicut sciverit seu poterit ultra convencionem suam praemissam. Et idem Johannes nullam (a hole in the deed) artium praedictarum a dicto Thoma apprenticio suo concelabit durante termino praenotato. Invenient insuper idem Johannes et assignati sui dicto Thomae omnia sibi necessaria, videlicet vistum suum, et vestitum, lineum, lectum, hospicium, calcementa et caetera sibi competencia annuatim sufficienter, prout aetas et status ipsius Thomae exigerint durante termino suo praefixo. In cujus rei testimonium partes praedictae hiis Indenturis sigilla sua alternatim apposuerunt. Data apud Norhampton, die Sabbati proxima post festum sancti Lucae apostoli et evangelistae, anno regni regis Ricardi secundi post conquestum decimo nono. Hiis testibus, Henrico Caysho, tunc majore villae Norhampton, Willielmo Wale et Johanne Wodeward, tunc ibidem ballivis. Ricardo Gosselyn, Johanne Esex Smyth, et aliis. (A.D. 1396)

INDENTURE OF APPRENTICESHIP FROM THE MERCER'S COMPANY'S RECORDS, A.D. 1414

From Hibbert, The Influence and Development of English Guilds, 52.

Haec Indentura testatur etc. inter Johannem Hyndlee de Northampton, Brayser, et Gulielmum filium Thomae Spragge de Salopia, quod predictus Gulielmus posuit semetipsum apprenticium dicto Johanni Hyndlee, usque ad finem octo annorum, ad artem vocatam brasyer's craft, quadictus Johannes utitur, medio tempore humiliter erudiendum. Infra quem quidem terminum praefatus Gulielmus concilia dicti Johannis Hyndlee magistri sui celanda celabit. Dampnum eidem Johanni nullo modo faciet nec fieri videbit, quin illud cito impediet aut dictum magistrum suum statim inde premuniet. A servicio suo seipsum illicite non absentabit. Bona et catalla dicti Johannis absque ejus licentia nulli accomodabit. Tabernam, scortum, talos, aleas, et joca similia non frequentabit, in dispendium magistri sui. Fornicationem nec adulterium cum aliqua muliere de domo et familia dicti Johannis nullo modo committet, neque uxorem ducet, absque licentia magistri sui. Praecepta et mandata licita et racionabilia magistri sui ubique pro fideli posse ipsius Gulielmi, diligenter adimplebit et eisdem mandatis libenter obediet. Et si praedictus Gulielmus de aliqua convencione sua vel articulo praescripto defecerit, tunc idem Gulielmus juxta modum et quantitatem delicti sui magistro suo satisfaciet emendam aut terminum apprenticiatus sui duplicabit. Et praefatus Johannes et assignati sui apprenticium suum in arte praedicta melioro modo quo idem Johannes sciverit ac poterit tractabunt docebunt et informabunt, seu ipsum informari facient sufficienter, debito modo castigando, et non aliter. Praeterea dictus Johannes concedit ad docendum et informandum dictum Gulielmum in arte vocata Peuterer's Craft adeo bene sicut sciverit seu poterit ultra convencionem suam praemissam. Et idem Johannes nullam partem artium praedictarum ab apprenticio suo concelabit. Invenient insuper Johannes et assignati sui dicto Gulielmo omnia sibi necessaria, viz. victum suum et vestitum, lineum, laneum, lectum, hospicium, calcaementa et caetera sibi competencia annuatim sufficienter, prout aetas et status ipsius Gulielmi exigerint. In cujus rei testimonium etc. 1414.

Transcript of an Indenture Preserved at Corsham, Wilts, dated Jan. 16, 1708

From Dunlop, English Apprenticeship and Child Labour, 352.

This Indenture made the sixteenth day of January in the seaventh yeare of the Reigne of our Sovraigne Lady Anne of Greate Brittain ffrance and Ireland Queene Defender of the ffaith ex Anno qo Dom 1708 Betweene William Selman of the pish of Corsham in the County of Wiltes Husbandman and Richard Selman son of the sd William Selman of the one pte and Thomas Stokes holder of the pish of Corsham aforesaid Broadweaver of the other pte Witnesseth that the said Richard Selman of his owne voluntarie will and with the consent of his sd ffather William Selman Hath put himselfe an Apprentice unto the said Thomas Stokes and with him hath covenanted to dwell as his Appntice from the day of the date hereof untill the full end and terme of Seaven Yeares fully to be Compleate and ended during all which tyme the said Richard Selman shall well and faithfully serve him the said Thomas Stokes his master his secrets lawfully to be kept shall keep his Commandmts lawfull and honest shall doe and execute hurt unto his said Master hee shall not doe nor consent to be done Tavernes or Alehouses hee shall not haunt Dice Cardes or any other unlawful games hee shall not use ffornication with any women hee shall not committ during such tyme as he shall stay in his Masters service Matrymony with any woman hee shall not Contract or espouse himselfe during the said Terme of Seaven yeares The goods of his said Master inordinately hee shall not wast nor to any man lend without his Masters Lycence from his Masters house or business hee shall not absent himselfe or plong himselfe by Night or by day without his Masters leave, but as a true and faithfull servant shall honestly behave himselfe towards his sd Master and all his both in words and deedes And the said Thomas Stokes doth for himselfe his Executors and Administrators promise and Covenant to and with the sd William Selman and Richard Selman his Appntice to teach or cause the said Richard Selman to be taught and instructed in the trade Art science or occupation of a Broadweaver after the best manner that he can or may with moderate Correction finding and allowing unto his sd Servant meate drinke Apparrell Washing Lodging and all other things whatsoever fitting for an appntice of that trade during the said term of Seaven yeares And to give unto his sd Appntice at the end of the sd terme double Apparell (to witt) one suite for holy dayes and one for worken dayes. In witness whereof the said pties to the psent Indentures interchangeably have sett their hands and seales the day and yeare first above written Sealed and Delivered in the psence of Thomas Stokes.

APPENDIX B

PRESENTMENT OF THE TOWN OF TOPSFIELD, MASS., FOR
VIOLATING THE ACT OF 1642

From Records and Files of the Quarterly Courts of Essex County, IV, 272.

Warrant to the constable of Topsfield, dated Mar. 2, 1668:
"Whereas the law published by the Honered Generall Court lib. 1, pag
76, doe require all Townes from time to time to dispose of all single persons and inmates within their Towns to service or otherwise and in pag.
16, tit. children & youth, It is required of the selectmen that they see
that all youth under family Government be taught to read perfectly the
english tongue, have knowledge in the capital laws, and be taught some
orthodox catechism, and that they be brought up to some honest employment, profitable to themselves and to the commonwealth, and in
case of neglect, on the part of famaly Governours, after admonition
given them, the sayd selectmen are required, with the helpe of two magistrates, or next court of that shire, to take such children or apprentices
from them, and place them forth with such as will looke more straitly
to them. The neglect wherof, as by sad experience from court to court
abundantly appears, doth occasion much sin and prophanes to increase
among us, to the dishonor of God, and the ensueing of many children
and servants, by the dissolute lives and practices of such as doe live
from under family Government and is a great discouragement to most
family governours, who consciently indeavour to bring up their youth
in all christian nurture, as the laws of God and this commonwealth
doth require;" said constable was ordered to acquaint the selectmen of
the town that "the court doth expect and will require that the sayd
laws be accordingly attended, the prevalency of the former neglect notwithstanding, and you are also required to take a list of the names of
those young persons within the bounds of your Town, and all adjacent
farmes, though out of all Towne bounds, who do live from under family
government viz. doe not serve their parents or masters, as children apprentices, hired servants, or journeymen ought to do, and usually did in
our native country, being subject to there commands & discipline and
the same you are to returne to the next court to be held at Ipswich the
30 day of this month, etc.; signed by Robert Lord, cleric; and served
by Thomas Dorman, constable of Tospfield, who returned that he had
made the selectmen acquainted with Mathew Hooker, who was all that
he found in the town."

BIBLIOGRAPHY

SOURCES QUOTED

ENGLAND

(Arranged alphabetically)

Archeological Journal. Vol. XXIX. London, 1872.

ATKINS, S. E., and OVERALL, W. H. Some Account of the Worshipful Company of Clockmakers of the City of London. London, 1881.

BATESON, M. (ed.). Burough Customs. Selden Society. London, 1904.

BIRCH, W. D. G. (ed.). The Historical Charters and Constitutional Documents of the City of London. London, 1887.

CUNNINGHAM, W. The Growth of English Industry and Commerce. Cambridge Univ. Press. Vol. I, Early and Middle Ages. Fourth edition, 1905. Vol. II, Modern Times, 1892.

DUNLOP, O. J., and DENMAN, R. D. English Apprenticeship and Child Labour. London, 1912.

FURNIVALL, F. J. (ed.). The Fifty Earliest English Wills. Early English Text Society. London, 1882.

HARRIS, M. D. (ed.). Coventry Leet Book, or Mayor's Register. 1420–1550. Early English Text Society. London, 1907–1913.

HIBBERT, F. A. The Influence and Development of English Gilds. Cambridge Univ. Press, 1891.

HUDSON, W., and TINGEY, J. C. (eds.). The Records of the City of Norwich. 2 vols. Norwich, 1906–1910.

JEAFFERSON, J. C. (ed.). Middlesex County Records. 4 vols. Vols. II and III. London, 1886.

JUPP, E. B., and POCOCK, W. W. An Historical Account of the Worshipful Company of Carpenters of the City of London. London, 1887.

LAMBERT, J. M. Two Thousand Years of Gild Life. London, 1891.

LEACH, A. F. (ed.). Beverley Town Documents. Selden Society. London, 1900.

Manuscripts of Beverley. Report of Historical Manuscripts Commission. London, 1900.

PROTHERO, G. W. Select Statutes and Other Constitutional Documents Illustrative of the Reigns of Elizabeth and James I. Oxford, 1906.

RILEY, H. T. Memorials of London Life, in the XIIIth, XIVth, and XVth Centuries. London, 1868.

RILEY, H. T. (ed.). Munimenta Gildhallae Londoniensis. 3 vols. Vol. I, Liber Albus. Vol. II, Liber Custumarum. Vol. III, Liber Albus, translations. Rolls Series. London, 1859–1862.

ROGERS, J. E. T. History of Agriculture and Prices. 6 vols. Oxford, 1866.

SCOTT, J. B. A Short Account of the Wheelwrights' Company. London, 1884.

SHARPE, R. R. (ed.). Calendar of Letter-Books Preserved among the Archives of the Corporation of the City of London at the Guildhall. London, 1899 1910 Letter-Books, B, C, D, E, G, H, I, K, L.

SHARPE, R. R. (ed.). Calendar of Letters from the Mayor and Corpora tion of the City of London, 1350–1370. London, 1885.

SMITH, L. T. (ed.). Robert Ricart, The Maire of Bristowe is Kalendar. Cambden Society. London, 1872.

SMITH, T. English Gilds. The Original Ordinances of More than One Hundred Early English Gilds. Early English Text Society. London, 1870.

STAHLSCHMIDT, J. C. L. Surrey Bells and London Bell-Founders. London, 1884.

STUBBS, W. (ed.). Chronicles of the Reigns of Edward I and Edward II. 2 vols. Rolls Series. London, 1882.

UNWIN, G. Industrial Organization in the Sixteenth and Seventeenth Centuries. Oxford, 1904.

York Memorandum Book, Part 1. Surtees Society. London and Durham, 1912.

YOUNG, S. The Annals of the Barber Surgeons of London. London, 1890.

NEW ENGLAND

(Arranged alphabetically under laws, town records, and other sources)

CONNECTICUT

Laws

HOADLEY, C. H. (ed.). Records of the Colony and Plantation of New Haven from 1638 to 1649. Hartford, 1857.

Laws of Connecticut, 1796. (Hudson and Goodwin, printers.)

TRUMBULL, J. H., and HOADLEY, C. H. (eds.). Public Records of the Colony of Connecticut. Hartford, 1850–1890.

Town records and histories

MANWARING, C. W. (ed.). A Digest of the Early Connecticut Probate Records, 1635–1750. 3 vols. Hartford, 1904.

STILES, H. R. The History of Ancient Windsor, Connecticut. New York, 1859.

Newspapers

Connecticut Journal, New Haven, Dec. 13, 1798; Sept. 4, 1799; Dec. 5, 1799. (State Historical Library, Madison, Wis.)

MAINE

York Deeds. Books I–XVIII. Portland, Maine, 1887.

MASSACHUSETTS

Laws

AMES, E., and GOODELL, A. C. (eds.). The Acts and Resolves, public and private of the Province of Massachusetts Bay. 1692–1780. 8 vols. Boston, 1869–1896. (I, 1692–1714; II, 1715–1741; III, 1769–1780).

SHURTLEFF, N. B. (ed.). Records of the Governor and Company of the Massachusetts Bay in New England. 1628–1686. 5 vols. Boston, 1853–1854.

WHITMORE, W. H. (ed.). The Colonial Laws of Massachusetts. Reprinted from the edition of 1660, with supplements to 1672, containing also the body of Liberties of 1641. Boston, 1889.

Town records and histories

Billerica, History of. Hazen, H. A. Boston, 1883.

Boston, Record Commissioners Report of, 22 vols. Boston, 1876–1890.

Braintree, Records of the Town of, 1640–1793. Bates, S. A. (ed.). Randolph, Mass., 1886.

Brookline, Muddy River and Brookline Records, 1634–1838. Brookline, 1875.

Cambridge, Records of the Town of, 1630–1703. Cambridge, 1901.

Dedham, The Early Records of the Town of, 1630–1706. Dedham, 1892–1894.

Dorchester, Town Records of, 1631–1687. Fourth reprint of the record commissioners of the City of Boston. Boston, 1880.

Duxbury, Copy of the Old Records of the Town of, from 1642 to 1770. Plymouth, 1893.

Lancaster, The Early Records of, 1643–1725. Lancaster, 1884.

Malden, History of. Corey, D. P. Malden, Mass., 1899.

Newbury, History of. Currier, J. J. Boston, 1902.

Salem, Annals of. Felt, J. B. Salem, 1845.

Springfield, The First Century of the History of. Burt, H. M. Springfield, 1899.

Watertown Records, 1634–1832. 3 vols. Watertown Hist. Soc. Watertown 1894–1900.

Diaries, newspapers and other sources

Boston Evening Post, March 9, 1747. (State Historical Library, Madison, Wis.)

Boston Gazette, or Weekly Journal, Tues., July 11, 1749. (State Historical Library, Madison, Wis.)

Boston News Letter, April 15, 1714; April 26, 1715. (State Historical Library, Madison, Wis.)

Diary of COTTON MATHER, 1681–1724. 2 vols. Massachusetts Historical Society Collections, 7th Series, Vols. VII and VIII. Boston, 1911–1912.

Diary of SAMUEL SEWALL, 1674–1729. 2 vols. Mass. Hist. Soc. Coll. Fifth Series. Vols. V, VI, VII. Boston, 1878, 1879, 1882.

Essex Institute, Historical Collections. Vols. I and II. Salem, 1859 and 1860.

Herald of Freedom, Boston, Tuesday, May 21, 1791. (State Historical Library, Madison, Wis.)

Note-book kept by Thomas Lechford in Boston, Massachusetts Bay, from June 27, 1638, to July 29, 1641. Trans. American Antiquarian Soc. Vol. VII, 1885.

Old South Leaflets. Vol. VII, No. 164.

Records and Files of the Quarterly Courts of Essex County, Massachusetts, 1636–1671. 4 vols. Essex Institute. Salem, Mass., 1911–1914.

The New England Historical and Genealogical Register. Vols. XXXIII and XXXIV. Boston, 1879–1880.

THOMAS'S Massachusetts or Spy Worcester Gazette, Worcester, Wed. Jan. 4, 1797; Wed., Jan. 18, 1797; Wed., Feb. 21, 1798; Wed., Feb. 28, 1798. (State Historical Library, Madison, Wis.)

NEW HAMPSHIRE

Laws

BATCHELLOR, A. S. (ed.). The Laws of New Hampshire, 1679–1774. 3 vols. I, Manchester, 1904; II, Concord, 1913; III, Bristol, 1915.

Records

New Hampshire Province Records, 1680–1692. New Hampshire Hist. Soc. Coll. Vol. VIII. Concord, 1866.

New Plymouth

Laws

BRIGHAM, W. (ed.). The Compact with the Charter and Laws of the Colony of New Plymouth. Boston, 1836.

Colony and Town records

DAVIS, W. F. (ed.). Records of the Town of Plymouth. 3 vols. Plymouth, 1889.

SHURTLEFF, N. B., and PULSIFER, D., and others (eds.). Records of the Colony of New Plymouth. 12 vols. Boston, 1855–1861.

Rhode Island

Laws

BARTLETT, J. R. (ed.). Records of the Colony of Rhode Island and Providence Plantations in New England. Vol. I. Providence, 1856–1865.

Town records

BRIGHAM, C. S. (ed.). The Early Records of the Town of Portsmouth. Providence, 1901.

Early Records of the Town of Providence. 17 vols. Record Commissioners. Providence, 1891–1903.

Vermont

Laws of Vermont. Windsor, Vt., 1825.

Revised Statutes of Vermont, 1839. Burlington, Vt., 1840.

New York

Laws

Colonial Laws of New York. 5 vols. Albany, 1894.

East Hampton Book of Laws. June ye 24th 1665. (N. Y. Public Library.)

Laws of New York, 11th Session, 1788. Printed by Sam and John Louden. (N. Y. Public Library.)

Laws of New York, 1691–1751. Printed by James Parker, 1752. (Columbia Univ. Library.)

Laws of New York, 1691–1773. Printed by Hugh Gaine. (N. Y. Public Library.)

Laws of New York, Jan.–Apr., 1775. (N. Y. Public Library.)

Laws of New York, 1784. Printed by Elizabeth Holt. (N. Y. Public
Library.)
New York Province Laws. Duke of York, 1665. (N. Y. Public Library.)

Town records

Dutchess County, Book of the Supervisors of, 1718–1722. Vassar
Brothers' Institute. Poughkeepsie, N. Y., 1908.
East Hampton, Records of the Town of, 4 vols. Sag Harbor, 1887–1889.
Flushing Town Records, 1790–1833. (Manuscript folio volume. N. Y.
Hall of Records.)
Harlem Records, II. (Manuscript folio volume owned by Title Guaran-
tee & Trust Company of N. Y. City.)
Huntington Town Records. Street, C. R. (ed.). 3 vols. Huntington,
L.I., 1887–1889.
Jamaica Town Records. 3 vols. (Manuscript folio volumes. N. Y. Hall
of Records.)
Newtown Town Records, 1663–1695; Newtown Records, 1700–1714;
Newtown Records, 1714–1753. Manuscript folio volumes. N. Y.
Hall of Records.)
North and South Hempstead, Records of the Towns of. 6 vols. Jamaica,
N. Y., 1896–1902.
Westchester Town Records, Aug. 6, 1664–Oct. 17, 1696; Westchester
Records, 1707–1720; Westchester Records, 1711–1730. (Manu-
script folio volumes. Pages not numbered in "Westchester Records
1711–1730." N. Y. Hall of Records.)

NEW YORK CITY AND COURT RECORDS

Abstracts of Wills (1665–1786) on file in the Surrogate's Office, City of
New York. 17 vols. N. Y. Hist. Soc. Coll., 1892–1908. N. Y.,
1892–1908.
City of N. Yorke Indentures begun February 19, 1694 and ends Jan.
ye 29th 1707. (Manuscript folio volume. City Hall of N. Y. City.)
Indentures Oct. 2, 1718 to Aug. 7, 1727. (Manuscript folio volume,
labeled "Liber 29." Library of the N.Y. Hist. Soc.)
Mayors Court Minutes, Nov. 13, 1674 to Sept. 21, 1675; Mayors Court,
Rough Minutes, Nov. 1680 to Oct. 1683; Minutes of Mayors Court,
Jan. 1717 to June 1721. 2 vols; Mayors Court Minutes, May 1722
to May 1742; Minutes of Mayors Court, Jan. 26, 1724 to June 1729.
(Manuscript folio volumes. Pages not numbered. Minutes en-
tered chronologically. N. Y. Hall of Records.)
Minutes of the Common Council of the City of New York, 1675–1776.
8 vols. New York, 1905.

Ordinances of the City of New York, 1707. (N. Y. Public Library.)

Records of the Court of Quarter Sessions & of the Court of Sessions, May, 1722 to Nov. 1742. (Manuscript folio volume. Pages not numbered. Items entered chronologically. N.Y. Hall of Records.)

Roll of Freemen, New York, 1675–1866; Appendix to Roll of Freemen, 1695–1774. N. Y. Hist. Soc. Coll., 1885. N. Y., 1885.

Newspapers

Dairy and Mercantile Advertiser, New York, Wednesday Evening, July 19, 1797. (State Historical Library, Madison, Wis.)

New York and Richmond County *Free Press*, December 21, 1833. (State Historical Library, Madison, Wis.)

The Daily Advertiser, New York, Friday, Dec. 19, 1788. (State Historical Library, Madison, Wis.)

VITA

Robert F. Seybolt was born at Kearney, N. J., February 25, 1888.

He graduated from the Curtis High School, New York City, 1905, and was a graduate student in the Curtis High School, 1905–06. He was a student at Cornell University, 1906–07; Dartmouth College, 1907–08; Brown University, 1908–11, receiving the degree of Ph.B. in 1910 and A.M., 1911; Columbia University, 1911–13; research scholar, Teachers College, Columbia University, 1912–13.

He was instructor in English, Technical High School, Providence, R. I., 1910–1911; assistant in Education, Brown University, 1910–1911; instructor in Education, University of Wisconsin, 1913–January, 1917; assistant professor of Education, University of Wisconsin, January, 1917–